JAPANESE AMERICAN CITIZENS LEAGUE
WATSONVILLE-SANTA CRUZ JACL
P.O. BOX 163
WATSONVILLE, CA 95077

To California State University, Stanislaus

In Appreciation

From Watsonville - Santa Cruz Japanese American Citizens League
2014

Twice Heroes

AMERICA'S NISEI VETERANS OF WWII AND KOREA

Portraits and Interviews by Tom Graves

Twice Heroes: America's Nisei Veterans of WWII and Korea
by Tom Graves

ISBN   978-0-9858308-0-9
HISTORY/MILITARY/VETERANS
1. Veterans — United States 2. Nisei
3. World War II   4. Japanese American History
Printed in China
Published in the United States of America

www.TwiceHeroes.com

Nassau & Witherspoon books may be purchased for educational, business or promotional use. For information, please contact Nassau & Witherspoon, P.O. Box 460146, San Francisco, CA 94146, 415-550-7241 or sales@Nassau-Witherspoon.com

NASSAU&
WITHERSPOON
Nassau & Witherspoon Publishers™
San Francisco
www.Nassau-Witherspoon.com

The soldier is the Army. No army is better than its soldiers.

The soldier is also a citizen.

In fact, the highest obligation and privilege of citizenship

is that of bearing arms for one's country.

Gen. George S. Patton, Jr.

Go For Broke!

442nd Regimental Combat Team motto

Acknowledgements

Publishing a nonfiction book is not a one-man job. There are advisors, editors, designers, fact checkers, proofreaders, supporters and cheerleaders. If the book includes photos, there are photo labs (Gamma in San Francisco is one of the best) and digital technicians. There are too many to acknowledge by name, but some must be.

First and foremost, my wife, Becky Saeger, who, in addition to encouraging me, endured over a decade of interrupted weekends, disjointed vacations and detours of hundreds of miles for me to "interview a veteran I'd like to meet." She has become an advocate for sharing *Nisei* history with those who know nothing about it, and she has come to know many of the veterans, although as they pass away she cautions, "We need to make some younger friends."

Ron Schreier, a wonderful photographer and friend with whom I have worked for 30 years, not only helped with the project, but made it possible. Although he met only a few veterans, he knew them by their portraits, referring to them on a first-name basis. "Here is Kelly's photo." "I just read over Henry's interview." Thank you, sir.

Geets Vincent read virtually every interview and made me a better writer. She is herself a journalist, librarian, teacher, editor, elder philosopher and repository of a lifetime of fabulous experiences, which she shared on many long drives across the desert. She is also my biggest fan. Her late husband, Stu, a decorated WWII veteran, supported my efforts, shared his own story and his Purple Heart.

Marty McReynolds, a highly experienced journalist, photographer and editor, brought his own perspective and talent to the project and guided it into the book you hold today.

Alice B. Acheson, long recognized as a leading figure in publishing, is much more to me: a great friend, advisor, confidant, willing ear and therapist. Her generous participation cannot be overstated. Her husband, Ed Greub, is wonderful in too many ways to mention.

Fran McManus, longtime friend, author and publisher, activist, traveler and mom. She does all things well. Gene Underwood, a quietly brilliant marketing man, added the perspective of someone with an informed worldview and sensitivity to what I set out to achieve.

Three individuals have encouraged my photography efforts for decades: Jim Bulger, Grant Peterson and Judith Joy Ross. We do not speak often, but I find frequent inspiration in their works and in our friendship.

In this book based on interviews, there are nearly 100 subjects to thank. They were generous with their time and memories. I thank them for sharing their experiences with me, and thank them once again for their extraordinary service to America. Hundreds more added their own thoughts and experiences in conversations, at the 100th and 442nd clubhouses, at reunions and the Friends and Family of Nisei Veterans' events, led by Lawson Sakai and Brian Shiroyama.

The Nisei VFW Posts of California made me feel like one of their own. Other groups and individuals did the same, including my colleagues in the Joe Rosenthal Chapter, USMC Combat Correspondents Association. Drs. Ellen Sawamura and Howard Kline were ongoing and dependable advocates for my work.

There are many others working to preserve veterans' history, including Susan Uyemura of Japanese American Living Legacy, Tom Ikeda at Densho, and the talented and dedicated volunteers at the Hanashi Oral History Project. These individuals go largely unrecognized and underappreciated. They do not do their work for fame or fortune, but for their commitment to our veterans and our country. I admire you.

Preface

Twice Heroes is a personal work, one that grew from a simple photography project into more than a decade of learning about men at war and the hardships of their families at home.

This is a book about people who lived through the history most of us only read about. They share their personal experiences, thoughts and wisdom as no history book can. No one's life deserves to be condensed to 1,000 words or less, but as part of the veterans' collective stories, each adds up to much more.

My late colleague, Marine Corps veteran Dennis Cavagnero, invited me to meetings of the Joe Rosenthal Chapter of the USMC Combat Correspondents Association where I met veterans of WWII and the Korean War. I was impressed with their individualism and their unique personalities that were not unlike the close friends I grew up with, except our young lives were not interrupted by war.

As a non-veteran — and non-Marine — I mostly kept quiet at these meetings, listening to the friendly conversation and studying the faces around the table. But I wondered, how could I, a photographer, share these personalities? Photos alone would not tell the story, so I decided on a combination of portraits and interviews.

When I asked Marines if I could interview them, most said the same thing, "I don't have much to say, but you really ought to interview this other fellow, he's a real hero." I would hear this hundreds of times over the next decade. But I started with the Marines, July 4th, 2001. That same summer I met my first Nisei veterans. I quickly learned that, like the Marines, the Nisei are special. They overcame two enemies and have a unique story that deserves to be told.

Over the next decade, I met and interviewed many veterans, including the Nisei, concentrating on veterans of World War II and the Korean War. Some of the men I met served in both conflicts.

These were the wars of my father's generation, and some people I've talked to suggest my father's story was what I was after all along. Like my dad, most veterans do not like to talk about war, and more than anything, they don't like to talk about war with their families. I've learned the more combat a veteran saw, the less he wants to talk. He wants to forget, to heal. This self-imposed silence can last for decades, until the veteran recognizes that his life will not go on forever. Then there is

an urge to pass lessons on to a younger generation, to share some history, some philosophy, to leave behind *something*.

Just as the older generation feels the need to leave something behind, the younger one seeks answers: What town was my grandfather from; what were your parents like; where were you when you heard about Pearl Harbor? Even for children who expressed no previous interest, when they see their parents have turned the corner toward mortality, these questions can take on great importance.

I have only provided historical context in the introduction and section openers. Others have written fine books covering the Nisei soldiers, the Internment and other aspects of Japanese American history. A few standouts are listed on the *Twice Heroes* website, www.TwiceHeroes.com.

The Nisei have another reason not to talk about the war years. That is the guilt many still feel from internment. Imprisoned for unspoken reasons and uncommitted crimes, many carry a sense of guilt and doubt, though they did nothing wrong. The guilt has been compared to that of rape victims' self-doubting questions: Why did this happen to me? What did I do wrong? The stigma of the Internment is a stench the Nisei can't completely wash off.

I am often asked about Japanese Americans who were interned during WWII: Are they bitter?

There *is* bitterness, but each person handles it in his or her own way. Some, as you might expect, are angry and cynical; others have tried to let an uncomfortable past recede. Some are philosophical, analytical; some voice an appreciation of the changes that followed Internment and the war, happy for opportunities for their kids and grandkids. They may talk about the Internment as unconstitutional, or about Redress, the official government apology, coming in 1993, the first time the United States apologized to anyone.

The human spirit is resilient, but we each have different levels of resilience and different ways of activating it. For a generation of Japanese Americans, there is a residual burden others don't have to bear. That burden, sometimes present as a level of suspicion, was a hurdle I had to get over before each interview. "How did you become interested in Japanese Americans?" "Why are you — a Caucasian — doing this?" When I told them I wasn't being paid for this work, they were more suspicious, more confused. My "work," which does not fit into a capitalist model, confuses many people.

Growing up Caucasian on the East Coast, I was unaware of the Internment, and truly unaware of any discrimination against Japanese Americans. Our small New Jersey town had only a few Japanese American families: I knew the Asanos, the Kishis, the Tamashiros. Mrs. Tamashiro was a fourth-grade teacher, but our schools did not teach about the Internment.

I learned about the Internment as I learned about Japanese American History, and I learned that through the lens of the Nisei Veterans. I recognized this as an enlightened way to share history: through peoples' experiences, rather than by memorizing reams of names, dates and places.

These interviews were usually in the veteran's home, and averaging one-and-a-half to two hours. Most of the time it was just the veteran and myself. Nothing was recorded. I took notes instead, which I believe is less intimidating. When things got personal, the subject might say, "Don't write this down," and he would see me put my pen down, and then say what he had to say. What came next was sometimes uncomfortable, but always enlightening. My portrait of the veteran followed the conversation. Follow-ups might be conducted over the telephone, via email or in person.

Most veterans don't talk about their experiences, and Nisei veterans are more humble and tight-lipped than any, especially with their wives and children. Surprising to me, they often said their children never *asked* about their service. Mine was often their first interview, and after halting starts, I frequently observed a certain sense of relief as memories were revealed for the first time in more than 60 years. As they reach the end of their long march, more veterans feel the need to share and leave some of their history behind.

Some are not yet there. One veteran agreed to an interview, only to call me back the next day and decline. He said he battled nightmares of combat for many years and did not want to risk our conversation bringing them back. I understood, and my request for sharing his story went no further.

Because these are not recorded, verbatim oral histories, but highly edited conversations, I developed a set of guidelines for better reading and comprehension. I tried to give the reader a few highlights of a long life and a sense of the person who had those experiences, something you might take away from a chance meeting and conversation. I made corrections to obviously misspoken statements. When someone would say, "December 7th, 1991," referring to Pearl Harbor, I changed the date to 1941. With few exceptions, I chose not to confirm or correct broad statements ("About a week later …") or specific ones ("I was wounded on the second day.") that do not affect the larger work and history. Sometimes a veteran would show me discharge papers or a written commendation affirming a medal, but I did not investigate those who did not. Exaggerations that may exist are between them, their consciences and their buddies. Some veterans have all but forgotten the war, because of age or by choice.

I use the word "he," because these veterans are overwhelmingly male, serving at a time before our armed forces included many women. I should also point out that I and others refer to them as Nisei, but some Japanese immigrants preceded others by decades, so a veteran may in fact be a third (*Sansei*), or rarely, fourth (*Yonsei*) generation Japanese American.

As we do not speak with the same precision we may write, I smoothed out quotes and reordered some sentences to provide clarity for the reader, always keeping the meaning of the statement and, when successful, the voice of the subject. I left out highly personal information, most of which did not pertain to the larger conversation. More importantly, and unfortunately, I edited out entire segments of interviews — sometimes very good ones — which were too lengthy or did not fit the narrative. Our conversations jumped around, as conversations do.

Memories evolve and fade — with combat veterans, sometimes for self-preservation. Still, sensitivity and accuracy were my guiding principles. However, I may have misheard or misinterpreted some statements, and because I took notes, there are certain to be scribbles and writing errors. Sometimes my hearing and writing were clear, but a veteran changed his story later on, either because of a shift in memory or a change of heart. Rarely did one veteran speak poorly of another, and in those few cases, he did not reveal the other's name, not wanting to shame him or his family. That said, *Twice Heroes* is my work. I stand behind its accuracy, and I apologize for my errors.

If I have a message for the Nisei and others of the Greatest Generation, it is this: Tell your story to your children. If a conversation is too awkward, write it down, dictate it, ask your grandkids to videotape you. But do it somehow, and do it now. One day the intimacy of that message will be all your kids have of you and they will cherish it more than anything else you could leave them. I would give most everything I have to spend one more day with my father — if I thought he would talk with me.

While most Americans are truly and innocently ignorant of Japanese American history, people overseas still remember the Nisei veterans' accomplishments. While lost on its youngsters, Japan's older generation appreciates the great role of Nisei linguists in post-war Japan. Survivors of Dachau remember liberators with Japanese faces in American uniforms — men whose own families were imprisoned.

Far from the lights of Paris, small French towns in the Vosges Mountains celebrate Liberation each October, marking the day they were freed from German occupation by men they still call "les Hawaiiens." French and American flags fly from roadside windows; a parade, crowds and speeches fill the town square in Bruyères. Honor guards and bands perform at monuments to the Nisei that dot the villages and the site of the Lost Battalion battle, filling the dark forests with the Star Spangled Banner and La Marseillaise, and small American flags mark Nisei graves among the thousands in the Epinal American Cemetery. I am witness to all that, and I predict citizens of the Vosges will remember the Nisei veterans longer than anyone.

On November 2, 2011, Nisei WWII veterans gathered at the U.S. Capitol Building to receive the Congressional Gold Medal, Congress' highest civilian honor. I accompanied my friend, 92-year-old veteran John Sakamoto from Sacramento. Sons and daughters and grandchildren were there, some tearfully learning about the Nisei soldiers' legacy for the first time. Newspapers in Washington and around the country carried Congressional Gold Medal articles that November, perhaps a prelude to the final chapter of this piece of history.

In *Twice Heroes*, I have tried to "put a face" to the men called Nisei Veterans. Here are their stories, as they told me, between September 2001 and today.

Introduction

The 20th Century saw man first fly, and first fly to the moon, construct and employ an artificial human heart, create human life in a laboratory and expand democracy and human rights. But sadly, the century will be defined by War.

The World War of 1914–1918 was called "The War to End All Wars" for the worldwide scope of its battlefield and the slaughter of millions that in the end accomplished little beyond bankrupting the treasuries and populations of its principal European participants.

World War II, 1939–1945, was perpetrated by a few insanely ambitious military powers — some would say by a few deranged individuals — and thrust upon the rest of the world. There were few neutral countries, few opportunities to avoid involvement, few places to hide. Warships and airplanes covered great distances, oceans no longer insulated nations from war.

The United States, remembering the brutality of World War I, and embracing a largely isolationist attitude, desperately dragged its heels as it was pulled toward the Second World War. War exploded in Europe in 1939, but even in early December 1941, America was not fighting. Its only involvement was providing food and war materiel to allies Great Britain, China and Russia, and the armed escorts for delivering those supplies.

America and the world changed on December 7, 1941, when the Empire of Japan attacked U.S. Navy ships and military installations in the territories of Hawaii, Wake Island and the Philippines, killing thousands of military personnel and civilians.

Isolationism was replaced by anger and calls for revenge, as America declared war on Japan the next day, and Japan's allies Germany and Italy days later. As if denying the inevitability of the coming crisis, America's military was inadequately staffed with men and machines. A peacetime draft of young men into military service had been instituted in 1940, but the U.S. military was not nearly prepared for war. By then, when war with Japan appeared imminent to American military planners, a survey found only 40 Japanese speakers in the entire U.S. Army, a level inadequate for the intelligence gathering and communications needs of wartime.

Few dates are as significant to United States history as December 7th, 1941, one long linked to two phrases: "A date which will live in infamy," as declared by President Franklin Delano Roosevelt as he urged Congress to declare war on Japan; and "Remember Pearl Harbor," a catchy song and also the nation's call to arms against Japan and allies, Germany and Italy, urging Americans to prepare, materially and mentally, for what was to come. "Remember Pearl Harbor" became the motto of the segregated Nisei 100th Infantry Battalion, an ironic choice for Japanese American men whose loyalties were questioned.

The bombing of Pearl Harbor, while fundamentally changing World War II and the history of our country, changed the lives of one group of Americans above all others. The Japanese attack incensed the public to all things Japanese, including Japanese immigrants, Issei, and their children, U.S. citizens, the Nisei generation. The 1940 census recorded 126,947 Japanese Americans, less than .1 percent of the continental U.S. population of nearly 132 million. California accounted for three-quarters of the total for the 48 states and was home to over 40 "Japan-town" communities.

Immediately following news of the Pearl Harbor attack, a longstanding military contingency was launched: Plan Orange. Part of the planning for a possible war with Japan was the perceived need to isolate America's Japanese American communities, arrest their leaders, and eventually move the entire population into isolation camps, a mass imprisonment referred to as the Internment, or the euphemistic "Relocation" and "Evacuation," to be administered by a new agency, the War Relocation Authority.

American-born Japanese American men of the Nisei generation had registered for the draft, and some were already in the service. Soon after the Pearl Harbor attack, Nisei were no longer drafted. Although they were American citizens, their draft status was changed to 4-C, "enemy alien," ineligible for military service. Japanese American men already in the military had their weapons taken away and were moved inland, far from the coast. This policy continued until 1943, when a limited number were allowed to volunteer for the 442nd Regimental Combat Team, a segregated unit, commanded by Caucasian officers.

At that time, two Nisei units were already in service, the segregated 100th Infantry Battalion, and the Military Intelligence Service (MIS), which was overwhelmingly Japanese American.

MIS linguists had been training since November 1941. They served throughout the war in the Pacific Theater in field units and in intelligence roles, saving many lives and speeding the end of the Pacific war. They next served in post-war Japan, in the Korean and Cold Wars. Their success led to the significant expansion of language training programs for the armed forces.

In June 1942, a Hawaiian Territorial Guard unit, mostly made up of Nisei, was re-designated the 100th Infantry Battalion (Separate) and entered combat in late September 1943. The men's aggressiveness in battle led to success but also many casualties, earning them the nickname, Purple Heart Battalion.

By 1943, successful lobbying of the War Department and the White House allowed Japanese Americans to enlist in a new unit, an expansion of the 100th Battalion, the 442nd Regimental Combat Team, or RCT, a single, segregated regiment commanded by Caucasian officers. Response from the Mainland was tepid. After all, most Mainlanders were confined with their families in the 10 sprawling internment camps scattered across the country. Nearly all Hawaiians were spared internment, and Hawaiian Nisei enlisted more enthusiastically, giving the new regiment a distinctly Hawaiian character. The 100th Battalion transferred to the Camp Shelby, Mississippi, training facility. Nisei serving in other Army units were sent to Camp Shelby, where Japanese Americans were housed and trained apart from other soldiers.

Advanced in their training, the 100th Battalion sailed overseas before the 442nd, landing in Italy and soon entering combat. They took heavy losses at Cassino against established enemy defenses manned by experienced troops, then fought to the north of Rome and in June 1944, met the newly arrived 442nd. The 100th was re-organized as the 1st Battalion of the 442nd Regimental Combat Team, but because of its extraordinary record, the battalion was also allowed to keep its original "100th" designation, an Army first. The combined regiment is sometimes referred to as the "100th/442nd" to recognize its original Nisei soldiers.

No one who has not experienced combat can begin to understand it. For the planners and maybe the newspapers, it is a series of arrows, usually red and blue, across a two-dimensional paper battlefield. To the soldier or the sailor, combat is what's in front of you, what's to your left and right, what's happening now and what might be next to come.

All this is most vivid to the infantryman. People are shooting at you. You are slogging up a muddy road in a cold rain, crouching behind a tree or lying wet behind a small pile of rocks or a mere bump in the forest floor. Or standing in a foot of frigid water in a hole you found, or more likely dug. The enemy is straight ahead, uphill and unseen in a forest like those in the mountains of France, where it is nearly dark beneath the October clouds and dripping pine trees. It is raining. When the shooting starts, you forget you need a shave, and mostly, a shower. You did not sleep last night. Your feet are numb now. You are wet, cold, achy, scared and hyper alert to any sound or movement. Mostly, you are wet.

And there is the sound, sometimes individual rifle shots and explosions, sometimes a continuous chaotic roar. The enemy's 88 mm cannon, 30 rounds of death per minute, explode around you and shatter trees above you. Men are showered with branches and hot shrapnel, wounding some, killing others. Trees fall near or upon other solders. Mortar rounds fly out and crash in. You hear the enemy machine guns, usually more than one. Men grunt and scream. Bullets bury themselves in the ground near you or crack by your head, aimed at *you*. It is personal. You hear your comrades' rifle rounds, but as you pull the trigger on your own rifle, the explosions are strangely subdued. Your attention is on the enemy soldier you see or almost see as you fire: one, two, three, four …

The 442nd RCT, an infantry regiment reinforced with its own artillery, the 522nd Field Artillery Battalion, and the 232nd Combat Engineer Company, all Nisei, soon sailed from Italy to land in the invasion of southern France. The unit re-entered combat in the rugged Vosges Mountains, on France's border with Germany, meeting fierce resistance from enemy troops defending the German border and a railroad line essential for their reinforcement and planned retreat. At a high cost of dead and wounded, the Nisei dislodged the enemy from mountain strong points, liberated French villages long occupied by the Germans, and rescued a lost battalion of American troops in a heroic action with a high human cost.

After the Lost Battalion battle, Nisei were transferred to southern France to guard the border with Italy, still occupied by the Germans. Between bouts of combat, the depleted 442nd waited for replacements from the United States. Replacements were often draftees, as the draft status of Japanese Americans had been restored to pre-Pearl Harbor status, making many young men, even those in internment camps, eligible for military service.

The 522nd FAB joined the 45th Division for its push into Germany, while the bulk of the 442nd RCT returned to Italy to fight against the enemy's fortified Gothic Line, the final German stronghold in Italy. Anchored by a series of towering peaks, the rugged Gothic Line had resisted repeated attacks by Allied forces. One black April night, the Nisei followed Italian partisans over narrow mountain paths to spring a surprise attack on the rear of enemy defenses on Mount Folgorito. After months of fighting, the Germans capitulated in 32 minutes. The 442nd fought north through Italy until the end of the war.

In their short time in service, the 442nd became the nation's most decorated military unit, with 9,486 Purple Hearts, over 4,000 Bronze Stars, and 21 Medals of Honor, in addition to other commendations from the U.S., France, Great Britain and Italy. The regiment became known by its motto, "Go For Broke."

Nisei were officially permitted to serve only in the 100th/442nd or the MIS, but some served through the war in other units. Ben Kuroki famously served in the Army Air Corps, flying in both the Atlantic and Pacific war zones. George Masuda served stateside in the 13th Infantry Regiment and Tak Obata was in Europe with the 101st Airborne Division. A separate and top-secret MIS section served with the Air Corps in the Pacific, collecting data about the atomic bombs.

In April 1945, the 522nd liberated portions of the Dachau Concentration Camp outside Munich. War in Europe ended with Germany's surrender in May 1945. The MIS fought on in the Pacific until the end of World War II, then continued to serve in post-war Japan.

The stateside War Relocation program had proven itself — legally, politically and practically — a bad idea. Some camps closed before the end of the war, others soon afterward. A new problem presented itself: how to resettle a vast population whose homes and financial resources had been upended years earlier. Amid Caucasian neighbors' protests against their return to the West Coast, families contended with threats, beatings, shootings and arson.

In West Coast cities and farm communities, Japanese Americans tried to resume their previous lives as best they could. Revived institutions and friendships, and holiday traditions began to supply some sense of normalcy. Relations with Caucasians were, at first, tentative; an uneasy peace ensued. In Hawaii, a Nisei bank was founded, veterans' clubs formed, and a new

political voice was born, leading to changes in government and the judiciary, and eventually to Hawaii statehood in 1959.

President Harry S. Truman ordered the armed forces integrated in 1948, and today, the 100th Battalion, 442nd Infantry Regiment lives on as an Army Reserve unit based in Honolulu. The 100th deployed to Iraq in 2005–2006 and to Iraq and Kuwait in 2008–2009. During World War II, no Nisei soldier rose above the rank of major. A number of Japanese Americans have attained flag rank admiral or general since then. Terry Shima, a 442nd veteran and president of JAVA, the Japanese American Veterans Association, says 43: 29 Army, 7 Navy, 6 U.S. Air Force, and one Public Health Service.

After the war, while some gathered with buddies for parties and reunions, many more tried to put all things GI behind them. Men suffered from debilitating trench foot and other combat injuries, both physical and mental.

"A lot of guys in our company had terrible problems with alcohol," one veteran confided.

Japanese American soldiers lie in graves next to Americans of every national ancestry. Some lie in vast national cemeteries near their battlefields in France and Italy. Nisei warriors of Atlantic and Pacific battlefields helped their community succeed as much as any small group of citizens might have done. They accelerated the acceptance of Japanese Americans and, in a sense, all immigrant minorities, into American society. Combining motivations both new and ancient, they fought for their country, their interned families and their honor. They won a battle against racism, benefiting all Americans.

On November 2, 2011, the veterans added one more medal to their dusty collections Seventy years after Pearl Harbor, the United States Congress awarded its highest honor, a Congressional Gold Medal, to the surviving World War II Nisei Veterans and to the next of kin of deceased veterans. In 2012, the French government notified veterans they were eligible for still another honor, the rank of Knight in the Order of the Legion of Honor.

The vets had been honored in the nation's capital once before, in July 1946, when President Truman presented their seventh Presidential Unit Citation. That day, he famously told the Nisei warriors, "You've fought not only the enemy, but you've fought prejudice, and you've won."

Twice heroes.

Remembering Pearl Harbor

"It all started with Pearl Harbor," many of the Nisei veterans will say.

Perhaps more accurately, "It all *exploded* after Pearl Harbor." "It," racism, had been there all along. Even though Pearl Harbor, on the Hawaiian island of Oahu, was all but unknown to most Americans, Japan's attack on American territory produced panic and fears of what might come next. The attack also unleashed Americans' vitriolic racism that until then lived mostly beneath a veneer of civility, especially on the West Coast, where the Japanese American population was concentrated.

The sudden fear of Japanese ships appearing off Los Angeles or Seattle was tempered by the prevailing assumption our new enemy, an "Oriental" one, was inferior to Westerners, to Americans. Victory over Japan was a foregone conclusion, as most Americans were unaware of, or unconcerned by, Japan's successful military expansion across Asia and its vastly superior military strength to our own. "The dirty Japs attacked us!" It was as much an insult as a threat. "We thought we would wipe them out in six months," World War II veterans confess.

Contrary to the population's collective surprise at Japan's attack on America's Pacific territories, the U.S. government had planned for the eventuality, compiling lists of leaders in Japanese American communities. Immediately after the attack, telephones began ringing in police stations and sheriff's offices along the West Coast. Within hours of receiving the news, FBI agents and local law enforcement officers were knocking on doors, arresting Buddhist priests, Japanese language teachers, judo instructors and community leaders, mostly men of the Issei generation, immigrants from Japan. In rural areas, local sheriffs knew the men they were arresting, and knew them to be productive, law-abiding citizens. But word had come down from the federal government and, with lowered voices and downcast eyes, they arrested the unresisting Issei.

"They took my father away and we didn't hear from him for six months," one veteran said.

Authorities, fearing sabotage and fifth column activities, confiscated radios and flashlights (presumed signaling devices), and weapons — including firearms, traditional swords and, in some cases, even kitchen knives. Official curfews and travel restrictions were to follow. Japanese Americans fired from their jobs after Pearl Harbor said it came as no surprise. Property owners refused to rent to them. Neighbors stopped talking to their former Asian friends. Along with the shame of the many arrests, the dissolution of Buddhist temples and Japanese schools and institutions weakened the community's spirit. Worse, shots were fired into homes and at Japanese Americans walking country roads. Bloodied noses became commonplace.

With social trauma came economic crisis. Family breadwinners were absent or unemployed, and the Federal Reserve in San Francisco ordered banks to freeze the accounts of Japanese Americans. How would loans be paid on cars and fishing boats, rent on apartments and farmland?

The Territory of Hawaii was nearly 50 percent Japanese American, and although there were orders to ship them to mainland prisons, Hawaii's Japanese Americans were spared mass incarceration. But community leaders were confined at places like Sand Island and Honouliuli on Oahu, and some were sent to mainland prisons. Those employed at military bases lost their jobs and the status of Japanese Americans, always near the bottom of Hawaii's racial caste system, fell further.

Newspaper columnists and radio personalities called for removing Japanese Americans from the West Coast or sending them back to Japan. So did the American Legion, the California attorney general and Pacific Coast farmers and fishermen who used the newly accepted racism to attack their competition. Japanese immigrants had proved highly productive farmers and successful commercial fishermen. If they were to disappear, perhaps the Asians' farm fields and productive fishing spots would be up for grabs.

A curtain of fear, disbelief and uncertainty fell on Japanese Americans. "What can we do? What will come next?" Some found comfort and faith in the American system of justice: Surely, these all were temporary measures forced upon them by wartime. The Japanese American Citizens League, the JACL, urged calm, but, understandably, many still seethed with anger.

Still others, especially the Issei who were not, and could not, become U.S. citizens, considered returning to Japan — and some did. Their children were terrified at the prospect. They knew little of Japan, and nearly all did not speak Japanese, only English. They grew up on baseball and football, Boy Scouts and the Pledge of Allegiance. America was their home.

They were Americans.

Lawson I. Sakai

"I felt I lost all my rights as a citizen."

Lawson Sakai was a college athlete in 1941, playing football and baseball at Compton Junior College outside Los Angeles. He was proud of his "new" car, a secondhand 1933 Ford Roadster, whose previous owner adorned it with black leather seats and custom paint. The Ford served him and his friends well for drives to the beach, to their games and on dates.

Incensed by the Pearl Harbor attack, Lawson and three Caucasian buddies marched into the Navy recruiting office, ready to enlist. There Lawson learned, like all Japanese Americans, his draft status had been changed to 4-C, Enemy Alien. Although an American citizen, he was not allowed to enlist. When the recruiter turned him down, the four friends walked out together in protest.

"I felt I lost all my rights as a citizen," Sakai said.

His family packed up and left for Colorado, outside the exclusion zone for Japanese Americans.

"On the way, we decided to visit friends at Manzanar, which was brand new. A young soldier was at the gate, we told him why we were there, he handed us a pass, and we headed over to the administration building to locate our friends. While we were waiting around, a crowd gathered and soon started telling us, 'This is a prison! You'd better get out of here while you can.' We got back into the car and drove out to the gate where the same soldier was on duty. We handed him our pass and drove away. We had been there less than half an hour. We were probably the only people to visit Manzanar and get out!"

In early 1943, Nisei became allowed to serve, and Lawson became one of the original members of the 442nd Regimental Combat Team.

At Camp Shelby, Mississippi, Nisei volunteers from the Mainland joined with recruits from Hawaii. While the Mainlanders were generally shy and subdued, the Hawaiians, the majority, proved boisterous and happy-go-lucky, and they loved their gambling and drinking. Fights between the two groups were common.

Col. Pence, the commanding officer, asked them, "How are you going to fight together if you are fighting each other?" Hawaiian recruits were sent to visit Japanese American families at the internment camps. Bus rides to the camps were typical boisterous, joking affairs. But on the ride home, the men were silent, having realized the Mainlanders had volunteered from those same bleak prisons. The camp visits became the turning point for the two groups. The men bonded further in combat, facing a common enemy.

"We fought well together," Lawson said. "We were closer than brothers. We had something you will never have again."

In August 1944, the Nisei landed in southern France. Their objective: Munich. The troops were trucked to northern France, then they marched. Northern Europe's October weather was horrendous, with a heavy overcast dark enough to make days like nighttime. In the cold and wet conditions, men often couldn't take off their boots for five or six days in a row. Many developed trench foot. The men marched through the mud and water as best they could.

"Up a hill, down a hill, up a hill," Sakai said, shaking his head.

Outside Biffontaine, the 442nd rescued the "Lost Battalion," soldiers of the 141st Regiment of the 36th Division, who had been cut off and surrounded. The enemy held three sides of the battlefield, forcing the Nisei to make a frontal assault and suffer many casualties. Much of the fighting was hand-to-hand. Lawson shook his head as he remembered.

"In combat — when people are getting wounded and killed — the toughest guys break down," he said. "The battalion did not get replacements for three, four, five months. We were getting depleted."

Wounded by a grenade during the battle, Lawson was bleeding all over and out of the fighting for eight or ten hours. He was soon wounded again when shrapnel from a tree burst hit him; hot metal ricocheted off a rib and to the front of his chest. Medics evacuated him by stretcher, jeep and then train to Dijon, where he spent six weeks in the hospital. Sakai got to know the medics well — he has four Purple Hearts.

"Several of our medics got killed," he said. "They are the real heroes."

After the war, Lawson married his college sweetheart, Mineko, whose father, Jimmy Hirasaki, introduced garlic farming to Gilroy, California, now the "Garlic Capital of the World." Lawson and Mineko raised their family in her childhood home, a handmade wooden house, brought from Japan to San Francisco for the World's Fair of 1936, and surrounded by large fields of garlic. Although thieves stripped the ranch during the Relocation, they spared the house. But the historic structure later burned to the ground in a midnight fire in February 2007.

Yoshiaki Fujitani

"After you shoot your five rounds, run like hell!"

From time to time, gray skies dropped rain (or "trade showers," as the TV meteorologists call it), keeping Manoa Valley a lush green. Clinging to an Upper Manoa hillside is an older home folks here refer to as a "mountain cabin." Inside, surrounded by his books, the Rev. Yoshiaki Fujitani sets an old photograph down on a table.

Faded and browned, the photo shows an older Asian man in a three-piece suit standing with a young Japanese American soldier in U.S. Army uniform. It looks as if it might have been a going-away photograph. The two men stand at attention before a background of sand and scrub. Their resemblance is clear.

The young man is Yoshiaki Fujitani at age 20; the older man, his father, Kodo, age 57. The photo was snapped outside the U.S. Department of Justice prison in Santa Fe, New Mexico, where the elder Fujitani was imprisoned with other Japanese Americans. His crimes? His birthplace and his calling: He was an Issei and a Buddhist priest.

"I was not allowed inside," said Fujitani, himself a retired Buddhist bishop. "I just remember the high wall and gate. They allowed Father outside for an hour's visit. After a two-year separation, I asked, 'Dad, how are you?' There was nothing else to be said at that time."

Fujitani paused as his visitor inspected the photo. The sound of light rain had stopped, replaced by an intermittent chorus of unseen birds.

"I'm one of the younger veterans, you know. I was 18 when the war started. I was in ROTC at McKinley High School, so they made me a squad leader at the University of Hawaii ROTC. We had never trained with our rifles. December 7th, first thing, we were instructed to put in the firing pins. Until then we didn't know they were missing firing pins.

"The ROTC became the Hawaii Territorial Guard and we weren't very well armed," he said, and smiled. "Springfield bolt-action '03 rifles from World War I. We were issued five rounds of bullets and at the end of the shift, one guy would have to unload the magazine and hand five rounds to the next man. We were told, 'After you shoot your five rounds, run like hell!'" He laughed.

The men served for about a month and a half, until "The Hawaii Territorial Guard was inactivated one day and reactivated the next, just without those of us who looked like the Enemy," the retired bishop said. "Our captain was a black fellow, Capt.

Nolle Smith, a highly respected senior and a star athlete at UH. When the Hawaii Territorial Guard was inactivated, he had tears in his eyes when he had to tell us.

"In April 1942, my dad, a Buddhist minister, was finally hauled in as an enemy alien. I withdrew from the Varsity Victory Volunteers, the V.V.V., to protest his incarceration, and I came home to take care of the family. We had eight siblings, and only my elder sister and I were old enough to work and make money. In October 1943, Sgt. Edwin Kawahara recruited me and I decided to volunteer for the MIS. I was still 20 years of age.

"After MIS Language School, I was assigned to Pacific Military Intelligence Research Section PACMIRS at Camp Ritchie, Maryland. A man in our outfit, 'Ike' Haruyuki Ikemoto, age 18, was one of the last to be killed in World War II, on August 14th, the day before the war ended, when a transport plane overshot the runway on Okinawa and crashed into the ocean. Ten MIS soldiers on that plane were killed.

"In October '45, after the war ended, we were sent to the Tokyo First Arsenal to collect documents. We picked what might have military value: war plans, fortifications, maps, charts or anything of historical value," he explained.

"Many of us, with just a little reflection, can realize a negative could become a positive. For our hardship in the Army, we received the GI Bill, and that was a lifesaver. I chose the University of Chicago and went there for five years. I met my wife in Chicago on a blind date. I continued my studies in Japan and was ordained a Buddhist minister, and then I returned to Hawaii. In 1975, I became bishop — it was nice my father got to see that."

Rev. Fujitani stepped outside and donned a pair of sandals to walk the few steps down to his yard. Once there, he pointed across the road.

"You used to see the whole valley before these trees grew up," he said. "A friend of my father's once visited here, saw this view, and made up a simple poem."

> *When I have time, I look at the mountain;*
> *when I am busy, the mountain looks at me.*

Ted T. Tsukiyama

"There was a sound of thunder that never ceased."

World War II veteran, attorney Ted Tsukiyama strode across his living room carrying a stack of legal briefs. "I'm still working," explained Hawaii's unofficial historian of the Nisei Veterans.

He seemed happy for a distraction from his work and proud to talk of the struggles during World War II. Ted fulfilled his part in earnest, with enough experiences to fill an entire book.

"I wore five different uniforms during World War II," he noted, then went on to list them: ROTC, Hawaii Territorial Guard, Varsity Victory Volunteers, 442nd, and the Military Intelligence Service, or MIS.

"The Sunday morning of December 7th, I couldn't see Pearl Harbor, but there was a sound of thunder that never ceased. The University of Hawaii Reserve Officers' Training Corps was called out that very morning, and within an hour of the attack, I was in uniform. We were each issued Springfield '03 rifles and a clip with five bullets. The ROTC was to form a skirmish line at St. Louis Heights, where there was a report Japanese paratroops had landed. We waited for five or six hours in the sun, but the enemy never showed. By 3:00 that afternoon, the governor converted the ROTC to the Hawaii Territorial Guard.

"We were the only ROTC unit in the nation to go on combat duty during World War II and earn a battle streamer — that because of the 'Battle of St. Louis Heights!'"

Nisei made up the great majority of the 700-man Hawaii Territorial Guard, which, according to Tsukiyama, prompted the Pentagon to announce, "Honolulu is Guarded by Japs in Army uniforms," instigating the dismissal of Japanese American guardsmen.

"The Guard was decimated," he said.

At the suggestion of local YMCA Director Hung Wai Ching, the former guardsmen volunteered to form a labor battalion, the Varsity Victory Volunteers, or V.V.V., which began working with the Army's 34th Combat Engineers, based at Schofield Barracks, and, according to historian Tsukiyama, became the first all-volunteer Japanese American unit to serve during the war.

Hung Wai Ching undertook a trip to Washington, D.C., explaining the loyalty of Japanese Americans — and their mistreatment — to both President Roosevelt and his wife, Eleanor. He then showed off the successful V.V.V. program to John J. McCloy, Assistant Secretary of War, during McCloy's inspection trip to Hawaii, and within a month, McCloy ordered the formation of a Nisei combat unit.

"Hawaii's original quota for the 442nd was 1,500 men, and was soon raised to 2,500. Instead, 10,000 of us in Hawaii volunteered! We disbanded the V.V.V. when we won the right to wear the Army uniform. Of 169 original V.V.V. members, 109 joined up and 26 went on to serve in the MIS," Tsukiyama said.

"While the 100th Battalion was at Camp McCoy, 58 or 59 men transferred to the Military Intelligence Service Language School at Camp Savage. I was in the field artillery at Camp Shelby when they began recruiting for the MIS. I wanted to stay with the 442nd, so I purposely failed the test. I gave an Oscar-winning performance! But there was a tap on my shoulder. 'Pack your bag,' they said, 'you are going to Camp Savage.'

"I never studied so hard! MIS was just *school*, morning, noon and night. We studied Japanese weapons, military structure and *hego*, Japanese military lingo. When I graduated in February 1944, they sent 100 of us for additional training in special radio communication interception. The others shipped out to every theater where we were fighting the Japanese."

Tsukiyama continued. "By December we were in operation in North India, and then we flew into Burma, to a place called Myitkyina, 60 days or so after it was captured. There we could still smell the stench of dead bodies.

"We eavesdropped on enemy fighter plane communications in Burma. Each of our earphones monitored a different airfield control tower. We did that four hours on and four hours off, 24 hours a day, moving south as the Japanese were pushed back, and by July or August, they were pushed out of Burma," he said.

"There is an apocryphal story of two Hawaiian soldiers standing guard duty after Pearl Harbor: The Caucasian soldier asks the Japanese American soldier, 'If the Japanese invade, who you gonna shoot, them or me?' That capsulized the plight of the Japanese American soldier. But their distinguished record of valor and loyalty and military achievement was the Nisei soldiers' answer to that question," he said.

"This war, at least, proved their devotion to their own country, and compelled the Nisei soldier to fight against an enemy of his own race, without any compunction. You might say this was a turning point in America's treatment of minorities. A great lesson was learned during World War II — at least I'd like to think so."

Thomas Ukichi Wozumi

"We were afraid of getting shot by our own men!"

Thomas Wozumi smiled as he described Alapai, the Honolulu neighborhood where he was raised.

"Bread peddlers came around selling bread for 10 cents a loaf, and many folks could not afford it," he remembered. "The bread man would cut a loaf in half and sell it for five cents — and people could afford that."

Wozumi sat in a veterans' clubhouse one morning, speaking about Hawaii, the days after Pearl Harbor and his service as an original member of the 100th Infantry Battalion.

"It's long gone, but Alapai Camp was bordered by King and Cooke Streets, and Kapiolani Boulevard — where the Honolulu Advertiser is now. Alapai sent 24 boys to the 100th or 442nd. My wife's family had eight girls, and many of them married 100/442 boys.

"We were drafted in March 1941 — and a lot of people don't know this — but many were sent to various engineer companies with men of all ethnic groups. After three months of training, 200 of us local boys went to the 3rd Engineers at Schofield Barracks. Our company commander, Lt. Harvey D. Fraser, is a great man. On December 7th, he was ordered to take the rifles and ammunition from us Japanese Americans. He refused. He called all the men together and told them he trusted us. Lt. Fraser led our company until we went to the Mainland in May 1942. He later became a brigadier general, a PhD and president of two colleges.

"On December 7th, our platoon was building a barracks at Mokapu Air Base, a seaplane base. PBY 'flying boats' were stuck in their hangars, and the bombing knocked the hangars down."

Fearing further air attacks, his company was ordered into the countryside near Waialua, where they slept on the ground, without tents, for months. During the day, they constructed gun emplacements from Kaena Point to Haleiwa. The enemy planes did not return, but Wozumi and the other men faced a new danger — their fellow soldiers.

"When winds blew the sugarcane leaves, making noise, the sentries fired at it. When an irrigation pump started, they started firing. Animals came around to eat Hawaiian plums that fell off the trees, and they fired at that. We were stuck in our foxholes. We were afraid of getting shot by our own men! We were there from December 8th to the end of May 1942.

"Before we went overseas, there were no speeches or photos, like the 442nd had. We left in secrecy. My daughter Carol was born May 25th, but I didn't get to see her until 1945, when I returned after the war," he said.

Wozumi served in a messenger squad, four or five men and a sergeant, relaying messages between the company commander and individual platoons.

"We used radios to communicate between companies — but the radios never seemed to work," Wozumi said. "We always stuck close to the company commander. Taro Suzuki was our own Japanese American company commander. Another, Sakae Takahashi, was an excellent commander, and he later became Treasurer for the State of Hawaii."

B Company had four Medal of Honor recipients, including Wozumi's high school classmate, Alan M. Ohata. Another soldier, Yeiki Kobashigawa, led the company through a minefield one night, crouching over to feel for tripwires he couldn't see.

"Yeiki was what you would call a 'man's man.' He earned a Distinguished Service Cross by leading his platoon and destroying four machine gun nests near Lanuvio, Italy. President Clinton upgraded him to the Medal of Honor," Wozumi said. "Yeiki died in April 2005."

Wozumi continued, "I was wounded twice, the first time when someone hit a mine. They flew a bunch of us wounded to a tent hospital in North Africa on Thanksgiving Day, so I missed my Thanksgiving dinner. The second time was at the rescue of the Lost Battalion. I was one of the 14 men in B Company that made it to the end. Two of us are still living, me and Albert Takahashi in Los Angeles.

"On a vacation in Europe, I saw Cassino completely rebuilt. Boy! We never had a chance there — one good friend lost his life, another lost his leg. On the trip, July 24th was my birthday and they gave me a bouquet of flowers. I took it to a British military cemetery and left it there."

Wozumi passed around a recent snapshot of himself with two Army friends.

"That's all that's left," he said. "We have many 'invisible' men now, who don't participate or go to the club, but when they die, we still buy them flowers.

"More guys are dying, but now there are fewer of us to send flowers."

Hiroshi Isogawa

"They said, 'We don't want no Japs.'"

Hiroshi Isogawa grew up on a farm in Pinedale, on the edge of Fresno, in those days an amiable melting pot of a dozen nationalities. Isogawa remembers, "Before the war, Chinatown was flourishing. The south side of Fresno was Germantown. Kearny Boulevard was Italian. The east side was Armenian — so was the town of Fowler. Kingsburg was Swedish. Germans and Russians lived over Biola way.

"We had moved over to Herndon, but we heard something was going on in Pinedale," he recalled. "We heard neighbors were hired for construction work."

Isogawa didn't know the neighbors were at work constructing the Pinedale Assembly Center, which would soon confine nearly 5,000 Japanese Americans. Another 5,400 would be jailed at the Fresno Fairgrounds.

"In the early part of 1942, I was 16 and out in my car one day, a Model A, when I saw a whole line of Greyhound buses full of Japanese American people from Seattle. I waved to them and they waved back. They had gotten off the train and were put on buses to the Pinedale camp. Right after that, our family was ordered to the Fresno Assembly Center at the fairgrounds."

Once confined, Isogawa and his family settled in as best they could. Internees filled all the jobs in the camp, besides the administration and, of course, the armed guards. Isogawa found a job as pot washer at one of the kitchens. One day before lunch, the head cook suffered a heart attack. Isogawa was soon cooking for 400 people.

"They told me to fix Salisbury steak for lunch. I said we don't have any steak. 'You have hamburger,' they said. We didn't have a pot washer, so guess who did that, too?" he joked.

By September 1942, the Fresno Assembly Center emptied, sending the family to the internment camp in Jerome, Arkansas, where Isogawa graduated from high school the following year. With his buddy, George Yamana, he headed for Ann Arbor, Michigan, and began working at the University of Michigan. Yamana went to register for the draft and Isogawa tagged along, even though he would not reach draft age for another three months. He registered, and was called up the next week. After basic training at Camp Blanding, Florida, he joined with the segregated 100th Infantry Battalion at Camp Shelby, Mississippi.

"The cadre was mostly Hawaiian boys. I was speaking Pidgin English in a couple months, and they all thought I was Hawaiian. They made me squad leader because I was tallest. One time an officer walks over and says, 'I understand all you guys are farmers,' thinking we were dumb and uneducated. I said, 'No sir.' I pointed to my squad. 'That man is a minister, that one's a lawyer, he's a dentist and he's an engineer. The rest are all college students or college graduates. Sir, I'm the dummy here because I am only a high school graduate.' After that, he had nothing to say.

"I got home in May or June 1946." He remembers that's when the American Legion turned him and other Nisei down for membership.

"They said, 'We don't want no Japs,' and that was the end of the American Legion for us." Instead, Isogawa and his older brother Frank were among 38 Nisei Veterans who chartered their own VFW Post in 1953.

Besides Frank, who served in the Signal Corps in Italy after the war, two younger brothers also served in the military. Ben was drafted in 1946 at the age of 18 and sent to the Army's Counter Intelligence Corps (CIC) at Fort Holabird, Maryland. Tom was drafted during the Korean War.

Isogawa found many Japanese Americans had not come back to Fresno after the war. Businesses closed, Chinatown faded away and Russian-town had disappeared. He worked on the family farm for a few years before starting a new career managing grocery stores, retiring in 1983.

But the energetic veteran did not slow down. He bought a dozen American flags to mark the graves of friends in local cemeteries. As the number of graves grew, he bought more and more flags, until the Girl Scouts and Boy Scouts signed up to help him. As a longtime commander of his VFW Post, he helped organize Memorial Day services and Veterans Day parades, and he still volunteers daily at the local Veterans Memorial Museum. He is also dedicated to caring for his wife, a fulltime job he manages ably and without complaint.

Arriving home from the museum one afternoon, Isogawa and his wife settled at the kitchen table, where he began quietly looking through 50 years of the Fresno Post's correspondence. Coming upon the original list of members from 1953, Isogawa read it and paused. He seemed surprised to realize they were all gone.

Robert Arakaki

"I saw that hinomaru, the fireball of the Japanese flag."

"My mother was 18 when I was born, the oldest of five children. We weren't rich, but we had plenty to eat," Robert Arakaki said from a kitchen chair in his home, which sits hard against a Honolulu mountainside. The mountains cradle the Palolo Valley homes like his. Steep hillsides shade the houses from the sun but, at certain times of day, enshroud them in deep shadow. Arakaki is a proud veteran of the 100th Infantry Battalion.

"When my parents first arrived here from Okinawa, both worked at the plantation where I was born, the Waipahu Sugar Plantation. I thought this was my future, too, on the plantation. In those days, they had a railroad from downtown, around Ewa Point, all the way to Kahuku, carrying pineapple from Waialoa. The railroad carried all the big equipment for the plantations. I started working pretty young, and found a job at a trucking company owned by Oahu Railway, moving military material from the pier to Schofield Barracks," he said.

"I saw several planes fly over our house that morning of December 7th, 1941, and I saw that *hinomaru*, the fireball of the Japanese flag. The planes assembled over the ocean and went in one by one — then we saw the smoke from Pearl Harbor."

Fears and rumors spread at once across the islands, Arakaki said.

"People asked what will happen to us, what will become of us? There was a rumor the water was poisoned. Are enemy troops landing? At West Loch, there was a big explosion and rumor of a Japanese submarine. Sentries were so jittery some cows got shot.

"When the war started, Japanese Americans were all made 4-C and couldn't be drafted. But what to do with the 100th soldiers? The Japanese American 100th Battalion was already in the Army, and for a while, they took their guns away. In 1943, volunteers were allowed into the 442nd, and in 1944, I was drafted. I am glad I served! Look at our opportunities — we would still be on the plantation. I thank Tojo for that!"

Once overseas, Arakaki joined others in a replacement pool from which men were assigned wherever needed.

"I might have gone to the 442nd, but I went to the 100th, and landed in France right about the time they were going back to Italy, for the last push: Leghorn, Massa, Carrara, and Alessandria — that's where we were when the war ended."

Once the war ended, Germans troops surrendered by the truckload.

"We processed them: Anything issued by the German army, they kept; anything personal, we took: pocketknife, camera, cognac, women's undergarments. They had young soldiers, and old ones, too, at least 60 years old. German POWs were very talented — cooks, bakers, tailors. They were human beings just like anyone else.

"During wartime you can't see the *enemy* as people, they are the enemy. But when we meet them, they are just like you and me. Every year we have a ceremony at Pearl Harbor. *Kamikaze* pilots come and meet Pearl Harbor survivors. They forgive each other. It is very emotional for them."

He said, "The 100th Battalion never operated as one group, or even as individual companies. The platoons moved independently. We were only together when we all pulled back, but even then, we didn't socialize much. We kept together by our squads."

The Battalion, however, retained its identity long after the war because the veterans, looking ahead, each paid two dollars a month from their wartime paychecks to establish the 100th Infantry Clubhouse. Arakaki guided the Clubhouse for several years as its president, and when the subject comes up, he cannot disguise the pride in his voice.

"I feel this place is sacred. Everyone who comes to our door has a purpose," he said. "Gen. Eric Shinseki always talks about his uncle who was in the 100th. Shinseki says, 'If it wasn't for the 100th, I would not be here.'

"Veterans have a different outlook from other people: You are here today, you may be gone tomorrow. If you survive, you are obligated to make the most of your life, obligated to family and friends. I feel I live a very fortunate life — never had much education, but I was very fortunate. I got to meet the Emperor of Japan — I shook his hand when he passed through Hawaii — and I got to meet Tom Brokaw.

"The bad things create good things — if you learn from them. Because of our sacrifice, that's what we have gained."

Bob Takeshige

"Do your best, even if it kills you."

It was a very hot day in Honolulu. World War II veteran Bob Takeshige sipped hot coffee in a corner booth of a restaurant a mile from his home. He drove there himself, and would drive himself home. He is 94.

"I've lived in this neighborhood for 80 years," he said.

He wore a cool, pink polo shirt and gray slacks, shiny black belt and shoes, everything spotless and pressed, and apparently new.

"My parents' families knew each other in Yamaguchi. My mother came here at age 18. My father signed a three-year contract to work at the Kawahui sugarcane plantation. Later, he moved to Honolulu to work at a hotel as a busboy and waiter.

"I was born September 4, 1916, in Waikiki. Way back then, Japanese people were pawns. 'Your future is on the plantation,' that's what they told us. They didn't treat us as human beings. We could only get menial jobs. They tried to keep us down. We couldn't vote because you had to pay a poll tax of five dollars. My parents were making $20 a month, and they had five kids. To work as a streetcar conductor, you had to be 5'9", so that meant no Japanese Americans. We had no access to money. Banks would not loan to us until after the war, when the Central Pacific Bank was started by Japanese American veterans of the 100 and 442," he said. "But I don't have any animosity toward the white people," he said. "If you hold a grudge it only hurts *you*.

"I worked at the best hotel on the island, the Royal Hawaiian, as a bartender when I was 19, and you were supposed to be 21 back then. I started at $40 a month and I learned a white guy started out at $135. Union leader Arthur Rutledge was the first to defy the Big Five, a group of powerful corporations that ran Hawaii. 'Join a union,' he said, and as soon as we joined, our pay went to $135."

Takeshige was drafted in June 1941 and assigned to the 100th Infantry Battalion.

"We were an all-Hawaiian unit, and they called us the Purple Heart Battalion. We knew we had to fight — that was our duty. We didn't talk about medals, but we thought, if we are going to die, we are going to take as many of the enemy with us," he said. "There was no stalemate. At each encounter, it was Go for Broke! We did that because we thought we were supposed to. That's the way we were brought up: 'Do your best, even if it kills you. Die, but don't shame us,' our parents taught us.

"Once you break the line there is no enemy, so we'd go for three or four miles. The first day of combat in Italy, the general came up to see what was going on, because we were moving so fast. Later, in France, we once broke through the front line in 45 minutes."

Takeshige recalled, "One day a replacement arrived. We didn't even have a chance to talk to him before a mortar shell came in. Everyone hit the ground, but he stood there and he was the only one to be killed. A guy in my platoon shot a tank, but his sergeant was too close and the explosion killed him. Another guy had built a nice foxhole. He went on patrol and returned to find a mortar shell had landed right in his foxhole. The infantryman has the hardest job — he does all the work and gets no credit. Soldiers lived because they knew what they were doing. But if your time comes, you're going.

"I went into combat and was wounded on the first day when an 88 hit the tree and a big branch fell on me. I had shrapnel in my back. I went back to the front at Cassino, was sent to the hospital again with frozen feet, and I told them I still had shrapnel in my back. When the war ended, I was in a hospital in Chicago."

Takeshige returned to Honolulu but didn't want to tend bar.

"You worked at night and had no time for a love life," he smiled. He then revealed a clue to his natty attire.

"Aloha-wear was just coming in, and I began manufacturing clothing. My company was named Holoholo Apparel. I did everything: deliver, sew, repair the machines. I worked 18 years without a vacation. At age 65, I retired, and then I had a heart attack," he deadpanned.

He sipped his hot coffee, eager to finish it and head home. He looked out into the familiar sunshine, but he remembered a different landscape.

"My frozen feet still bother me," he sighed.

Don Masuda

"Every hour seemed like forever."

"I joined the Army from a relocation camp in Heart Mountain, Wyoming," said Don Masuda. "I'm a 100th Battalion veteran, from Anzio on."

Masuda grew up a Mainlander, but he's lived in Hawaii since 1967, when he came for a veterans' reunion, and stayed. Like other Japanese Americans from the West Coast, he and his family were interned in 1942, and memories of confinement remain as poignant to him as those of the combat he survived in France and Italy.

"In L.A., certain neighborhoods went to Heart Mountain," he said. "We are from East L.A., where there were Jews, Mexicans, Russians, Japanese. We never felt any racial resentment. There were two of us kids — my brother served in the Korean War. My mother was running a hotel in Little Tokyo. My father died in 1938.

"I knew sooner or later there was going to be a war, and Sunday, December 7, we were listening to the radio and heard the news. Soon, the American Legion, and newspapers and radio commentators were saying all sorts of anti-Japanese stuff. The Japanese American Citizens League, JACL, started way before the war. Japanese Americans couldn't own land and there was no citizenship for our parents. The fact that we had the *Citizen* in the JACL name is significant — something I never thought about before."

He paused before continuing.

"I was only 16. I didn't graduate from my own school, but we had a graduation ceremony at Santa Anita race track, where they sent us before Heart Mountain," he remembers. "I *had* to volunteer. We were locked up in a camp and I wanted to show we were loyal. I felt if we didn't do something, they might get us kicked out of America altogether. I went in August 1943. Maybe I was too young to go earlier, because I remember I had to get my mother's signature to enlist. She understood, she was pro-American," he said.

Masuda was inducted and sent for physicals and examinations. He scored high enough on one technical exam to serve in the Air Corps, although he quickly learned Nisei were only allowed into the infantry.

"I was on the train to the Air Corps and an Army sergeant pulled me off and says, 'Where in the hell are you going?' I learned that's what the Army was like! But the 100th was not like the rest of the Army — guys didn't want promotions, they turned them down. Or medals. One guy threw his medal back at the officer. The Hawaiian soldiers were from the plantations, where everybody is the same, and they didn't want to be better than the others," he said.

"Basic training? I didn't finish it. Instead, they sent me with half of my training company to the 100th. I didn't know anything, I just did what the other guys did. The 100th had just gotten over the worst battles — Cassino, Salerno, Benevento — these were the names I heard. The old-timers showed us everything, and we listened to them. Maybe that's the Japanese way, the older teaching the younger."

Masuda remembers the fighting in the Vosges Mountains, Bruyères and Biffontaine; battling the tree bursts and bad weather.

"We lost so many guys at the Lost Battalion battle, at one point I had to handle a machine gun. I didn't have any training on it, but there was no one else," he said.

"Combat is hard to explain. It's really hard, scary, cold and wet; shells bursting in the trees, losing people killed and hurt — plain scary, miserable feelings. Was I a veteran after the Vosges? Yes. Only because I survived. After the Lost Battalion, I was about the only guy left in my platoon. I was lucky, I only have a little injury from combat at Anzio.

"When the Russians were coming close to Berlin, it looked like the war was going to be over. An officer asked if guys want to go to Japan as interpreters. I didn't think my Japanese was very good, because I hadn't spoken it in a while. But I thought it was better to go as an interpreter than as an infantryman."

Soon however, Masuda accumulated enough points for a discharge.

"Civilian or Army? That's an easy choice! We were all tired, we lost a lot of men, and no one wanted to be in the Army at that point. My family was out of camp and I met them in Chicago, where I worked jobs at warehouses and the railroad, unloading produce from California.

"We didn't spend that much time in combat," he said. "But it seems I was there for ages. Even today, when I count the days, I think, is that all the time we were there? But every hour seemed like forever."

Bernard Akamine

"Look and learn."

Bernard Akamine held up an old but otherwise unremarkable five-dollar note from the Federal Reserve Bank of San Francisco. Unremarkable, except for the word **HAWAII** stamped boldly on the bill, front and back.

"In the middle of '42, we had to turn in our currency and exchange it for this," explained the Honolulu native and World War II veteran. "If Hawaii was invaded, we did not want the Japanese to get ahold of the real money."

Hawaii's new currency was one of many changes after December 7th, when martial law ruled the Islands. Some changes began earlier, as military and private contractors began enlarging bases, improving infrastructure and building defenses against a feared seaborne invasion. Dirt roads were widened and paved, airfields improved. Water towers were built, as were radar and communications stations and bomb shelters, and a perimeter defensive line of pillboxes sprang up along the beaches. Defenses were constructed on the outer islands as well, but the work concentrated on Oahu, home to Honolulu and Hawaii's principal military bases, Schofield Barracks and Pearl Harbor.

Akamine ran a hand through his thick, white hair and carefully put the special bill away. He had been a late replacement for the 100th Infantry Battalion, arriving in Italy near the end of the war. While he spoke of the Battalion's distinguished history, he talked more about his role in Hawaii's preparation for war, and as a perceptive observer, he described a few revealing human interactions he saw and still remembers.

Born in 1922, Akamine spent little time in high school before going to work for an electrical contractor building defense projects. What made him qualified to work in the electrical trade? He smiled.

"You look and you work — *Minarai*, the Japanese call it — look and learn."

Construction jobs were plentiful, and in February 1941, he went to work for a consortium of five companies building military airfields. Work continued around the clock constructing buildings with 10-foot thick walls, 25 feet underground. Cement mixers operated nonstop, hoping to beat an invasion the men prayed would not come. By December 7th, Akamine was working at the Wahiawa Naval Radio Station, a secret mountainside facility in a remote part of Oahu, where construction of two underground bombproof buildings was underway.

"They had asked us to work that day, the seventh, which was unusual for a Sunday. We reported at seven in the morning. There was one specialist, Jim, who spliced underground cable. He always parked his car nearby and ran a speaker into the manhole so he could listen to the radio while he worked. Jim came up, yelling, 'Pearl Harbor has been bombed!'

"Navy personnel had arrived a week before. We went over to the base commander's house, and a Navy lieutenant commander opened the door in his pajamas. He said, 'We will probably not be attacked, but better take your men to the bombproof building.'"

What happened next is a reminder humor and humanity do not completely disappear in times of war.

"There were 50 guys in there and not a lot of air. The mood was awfully tense, so I went outside to get some air and sat under some stairs with another guy, who was deaf. He suddenly became very agitated and started pointing up at the staircase. Civilians began heading down into the big bombproof building, and we saw some of the women had rushed out in their housecoats and nighties but without their panties. When we re-entered the building, we were laughing hysterically," Akamine said. "The other men came over and asked us what happened. We had to tell them, and then everyone started laughing, and that broke the ice."

A week later, Akamine drove with a friend to inquire about the man's brother stationed at Schofield Barracks. While looking around for the soldier, they saw a long trench in the base cemetery, a mass grave, and next to it, a pile of crosses.

"We found a cross with the brother's name on it," Akamine remembered. "My buddy stuck it in the ground and started crying."

Akamine went overseas with a group of replacements, reaching the 100th Battalion in March 1945, fighting in the Gothic Line and Po Valley Campaigns. Only a few months removed from the lush paradise of Hawaii, Akamine was struck by Italy's devastated cities, the waves of refugees and the immeasurable human suffering he witnessed.

"Every day, thousands of displaced people walked the streets, trying to go home. The Italians surprised us by asking, 'Where is the food you promised?' We found out later our planes had dropped leaflets in every village: *Advancing Allied troops. Help them and we will give you aid.* But at the time, we didn't know what the people meant."

Matsuji "Mutt" Sakumoto

"Our whole life actually changed right there."

"This is sugarcane land, right here." Veteran Matsuji "Mutt" Sakumoto gestured from his chair in the shade beside his house a few miles from the beaches of Oahu's famed North Shore. "I bought this land for $3,400 back in the 1950s. Waialua Sugar closed in the 1990s — all the sugar mills were closing," he said.

"I don't have an English name," he explained. "One day my brother said, 'I'm going to call you Mutt,' and I carried that name all through my life. There was a Japanese American ballplayer with the same name as mine. My brother liked the name and gave it to me. You know, I wonder what happened to that ballplayer?"

Sakumoto is well-practiced in the island art of "talking story," sitting with buddies and talking to pass the time. This day, iced tea sat on the picnic table; in his younger days, it likely would have been beer. Trade winds pushed the hot, thick air through the cluster of modest houses, a thankful relief from the afternoon sun. At times, one of his sons joined him at the table. Sakumoto has spent his life here, surrounded by the dark green fields, walking the red dirt roads, vistas of rolling cane fields punctuated by the mountains and the sea and sky, his time in this Paradise only interrupted by a war that started on a sleepy Sunday morning.

"Come 1941, I was a senior in high school," he began. "That Saturday night, we were down at Haleiwa beach, seven or eight of us sitting around drinking beer, telling story. About seven or eight in the morning, one fellow suggested we go for a drive. We were all drunk, and I said no, let's go home. So I was still in bed, sleeping, and I heard my mother saying in Japanese, 'So many planes. Where did they all come from?' I got up at 9:00 and walked to the gym, and everybody was talking story. I asked, what's going on? And they said, 'You don't know anything about it?' Our whole life actually changed right there," Sakumoto said.

"Come January or February, there was talk about forming a Japanese American outfit, all volunteers. I decided right there, and we all joined! We marched to Iolani Palace in Honolulu where all the big shots gave a good talk. Then we sailed on the SS Lurline. There was no escort, and we zigzagged as soon as we left the harbor. You had to go all the way down to D deck for chow, but when I got finally there, I couldn't eat, I was so seasick.

"At Shelby, we spent about two years training. I think our training was really extensive, because we learned everything, and I was fit to be an infantryman at the end."

Seasickness plagued Sakumoto again on the troop ship to Europe, and he dropped down to 110 pounds, but he recalls an inspiring part of the journey.

"There were big crap games all night. When a couple guys went up on deck for air, they ran back to get us. As far as you can see — left, right, behind — ships, ships, ships! The convoy had formed up. At Gibraltar, we saw them move into single file to sail through the Strait and then spread out again."

Talk turned to the fighting in the Vosges Mountains, where the Nisei rescued the Lost Battalion. A rifleman with the 442's I Company, he is acknowledged as the first man to reach the surrounded soldiers. Like most heroes, Sakumoto finds the notoriety a bit uncomfortable. In fact, as he talked story, his role in the rescue did not come up.

"In the forest, you can't see for the trees. The enemy was right there." Sakumoto pointed to a spot a dozen feet away. "He can't see you, but if he shoots, he can't miss. We took the village of Bruyères, and the people opened their houses to us. We got to sleep in their beds, sleep in the clean sheets," he remembers.

The aging veteran sipped his drink and thought back to the 442nd's first days in Italy, when more than once, the new soldiers found themselves dependent on their battle-wise brothers in the 100th Battalion.

"Our first day in combat we got pinned down, but after a while it got real quiet, and we moved out. At the first turn in the road, an American tank was burning. Around the turn, a German tank was knocked out, and for the next 10 miles we saw knocked-out vehicles and dead Germans. The 100th had been there the night before, cut off the Germans and killed them all," he said, remembering the grim scene.

"All *we* had to do was march."

Norman S. Ikari

"About 99 percent of the people in Ohio had never seen an Asian before."

"It all came to an end with Pearl Harbor," said Dr. Norman S. Ikari, talking about his civilian life but, at the same time, describing the end of his childhood and the beginning of a dark period for America and Japanese Americans.

Ikari was born in Seattle, but his family moved to Southern California in 1930 when his father relocated his dry cleaning shop to Montebello, a town a few miles east of Los Angeles. It was there Ikari first encountered discrimination.

"The landlady came out of the house in tears, crying, 'The neighbors don't want a Japanese family in this house,' and that was the first time I saw my mother cry."

There were limited opportunities for the Nisei, even for college graduates — work on farms, fruit and produce stands. Ikari finished high school in 1936 but, lacking funds, it would be three years before he could begin college. Instead, he went to a school in Los Angeles to learn chick sexing, a skill valued by chicken breeders. He then moved to northwest Ohio to work at several hatcheries. It was exhausting work, but he made lots of money. And, he said, "About 99 percent of the people in Ohio had never seen an Asian before. There were lots of questions."

Ikari then started college but was able to finish only a year before being drafted 44 days after Pearl Harbor. He was halfway through basic training when Executive Order 9066 was issued, shutting off Japanese Americans from military service and relocating many to internment camps. Ikari's family was split up and sent to camps in Arizona, Arkansas and California. His father returned to Japan. A younger brother, Ted, lived outside the exclusion zone in Colorado, avoiding internment.

Ikari was assigned to the Medical Replacement Training Center at Camp Grant, Illinois.

"No weapons training and not a damn gun in the camp," he said.

In February 1943, FDR and his Secretary of War Henry Stimson authorized the formation of a Japanese American Army unit. By November, Ikari transferred to the all-volunteer 442nd, losing his sergeant's stripes and seniority in the process.

"June 26, 1944, the 442nd was first ordered into combat. Our first objective: Belvedere, a little town in an enemy occupied area of Italy. The 2nd and 3rd Battalions were to attack, the 100th Battalion was in reserve. When the attack on Belvedere bogged down, they sent in the 100th."

Next came Hill 140. Ikari was the No. 2 point man in George Nukushima's squad, and Lt. Bryan, their young platoon leader, urged the platoon forward.

"We only went 40 yards or so and I got hit in both legs — like a lead pipe or baseball bat had hit me in both legs. I lay still for a few moments. I was blacking out, I had a hole in my leg. I heard footsteps and mortar shells coming in. It was medic Kelly Kuwayama. To this day, I remember every word Kelly said to me. First thing, 'Why didn't you put on a tourniquet?' Mortar shells bracketed us. Kelly said, 'We're taking an awful chance.' Next thing I knew I was being carried back. George Nukushima was bending over me. I was weak and in great pain. Litter bearers carried me a long way. I woke up again in a tent — a battalion aid station."

An ambulance took Ikari to the 56th Evacuation Hospital, where both legs were wrapped in a cast up to his waist. Between his legs ran a wooden slat the orderlies used as a handle when they lifted him. He received transfusions around the clock as a C-47 hospital plane carried him to the 6th General Hospital in Rome. An ambulance train took him to the 21st General Hospital in Naples where he spent several months.

He was later transported back to the States and, along with other 442nd and 100th veterans, assigned to Camp Ritchie in western Maryland. They were told they would wear Japanese army uniforms, to portray enemy soldiers at the Infantry Replacement Training Center.

"No way we were going to do that!" Ikari said.

Fortunately, the war ended before the men were faced with refusing a direct order. Ikari considered re-enlisting but, instead, finished his degree at UCLA under the GI Bill and went to work at the National Institutes of Health in Washington, D.C. He attended graduate school at the same time, earning a Master's and a PhD.

His kid brother, Ted, had enlisted and served in the 522nd Field Artillery Battalion, the regiment's artillery arm. His brother, Bob, took Japanese language training at Fort Snelling, Minnesota, and served in the CIC section of the MIS. Bob requested to be assigned to northern Japan where he found their father.

"Father was glad to see him but did not want him around," Ikari said.

Lloyd Fujitani   442nd Regimental Combat Team   World War II

Masato Yamashita   442nd Regimental Combat Team   World War II

Bones Fujimoto   442nd Regimental Combat Team   World War II

Mits Hayashi   442nd Regimental Combat Team   World War II

Tsutomu Oi   1399th Engineer Battalion   World War II

Thomas Shigeru Ooka   442nd Regimental Combat Team   .   World War II

Jack Oda   442nd Regimental Combat Team   World War II

Leo Morishita   100th Infantry Battalion   World War II

Terry Shima   442nd Regimental Combat Team   World War II

Yukio Sumida   442nd Regimental Combat Team   World War II

Knowing the Enemy

There's an adage attributed to Napoleon, "An army marches on its stomach."

But no army advances, no navy sails, no airplane takes off or single cannon is fired without knowing the location of the enemy. This requires "military intelligence" obtained through spying, interception of messages, interrogation of prisoners — all techniques that have been employed for centuries. Essential to these efforts is the ability to understand the enemy's language.

Japan, an island nation with a closed, feudal society, long considered its seas and its unique language as assets, as shields against foreigners. But it began to loosen its isolationist philosophy in the 1860s and enter trade and diplomatic relations with other countries. Communicating with foreigners became necessary. Missionaries, businessmen, diplomats and scholars studied and began to speak Japanese. A crack in the language shield developed.

As Japan developed into a modern nation, its military developed as well. A powerful Imperial navy defeated the Russians in 1905; the army had fought much larger China to a standstill a few years earlier. By the 1930s, Japan's military held sway over the fledgling nation. A second war with China sought to expand Japanese territory and its status in Asia and beyond. American leaders carefully watched this expansion. The United States had its own territories in the Pacific, the largest being the Philippines.

Japanese immigration to the U.S. began in the late 19th century. Field workers were needed in Hawaii and on the U.S. mainland at the same time Japan sought to expand its relationship with the West.

Laborers were also needed on farms, railroads and lumber camps in the American West. With its largely agricultural economy, California in particular needed workers willing to do the tough jobs of clearing land, planting and picking crops, all for low wages. Male workers put some of their wages aside and married "picture brides," women from Japan they knew only from the small black and white portraits matchmakers showed them. American-born children from these marriages were, by law, American citizens.

The Issei held on to their language (English was as hard for them as Japanese is to English speakers), foods and traditions as best they could. And they shared them with their children, hoping to preserve their heritage. One way of imparting the culture was to send children to live with relatives in Japan and attend school there, improving their language skills and learning about things Japanese. These were the *kibei*, mostly high-school age (and sometime younger) boys, who would spend their school years in Japan before returning to the U.S., and return speaking excellent Japanese.

By 1940, Japanese expansionist ambitions and its powerful military began to threaten Western interests in Asia. The Axis Alliance had already linked Japan and Italy with the rising threat from a Nazi Germany. However, unlike the German and Italian languages, studied and spoken in the U.S., Japanese speakers were rare. The military recognized such a gap in its military intelligence capabilities would be a great disadvantage if America went to war with Japan.

The Army undertook a program to identify Japanese-speakers and establish a school to train more. Professors, businessmen and others — nearly all Nisei — were quietly recruited for the project. A single classroom was set up in the Presidio of San Francisco in a derelict aircraft hangar called Building 640. The Military Intelligence Service Language School (MISLS) was classified Top Secret. Sixty students and their instructors lived and studied, isolated from the rest of the base. They marched to meals, ate together and marched back without socializing or speaking to other soldiers. Students began a regimen of six-days-a-week courses and accompanying extensive homework, learning to write and speak Japanese, as well as the technical terms and jargon of the enemy's military. They began their studies in November 1941. The war started a month later.

The nation and the military were shocked into action by the Pearl Harbor attack. The MISLS accelerated its classes. Students understood the urgency of their mission. Their country had been attacked, their role now deadly serious. They worked constantly, using flashlights to study under the covers or in the latrine after lights out.

Their study was disrupted in the spring of 1942. Maj. Gen. John L. DeWitt, Commander of the 4th Army and the Western Defense Command, infamously undertook the forced relocation of Japanese Americans, his prerogative under President Franklin Roosevelt's Executive Order 9066. Orders came from his nearby Presidio office for the Nisei linguists to comply with other Japanese Americans and move away from the West Coast.

The language school was moved to an old Army camp outside Minneapolis, where some men saw snow for the first time. Camp Savage was in poor condition. MISLS students occupied a former homeless men's shelter. Coal-burning stoves had to be fed all night to take the sting off the Minnesota winters. But the studies continued. The school moved to larger (and better) facilities at nearby Fort Snelling in 1944. Hundred of linguists were trained. Men were deployed to nearly every American, Australian and Canadian force in the Pacific; others served stateside and some became MISLS instructors. Women served later in the war. Most, but not all, of the MIS soldiers had taken basic training; a few were not even in the Army, but civilians.

In addition to enemy fire, Nisei linguists in combat forces worried about being shot in combat by their own men, or men from other units in the chaos of battle. They worried about capture and the treatment they might receive. And they feared facing a former Japanese schoolmate or relative on the battlefield.

MISers could monitor radio transmissions and translate the messages. In one famous instance, intercepted messages enabled the Americans to ambush an enemy plane carrying Admiral Yamamoto, architect of the Pearl Harbor attack. American fighters shot down Yamamoto's plane, killing him.

Richard Sakakida was in the Army before the language school was created. He became a successful MIS agent working undercover in the Philippines, sending back intelligence information even after being captured by Japanese forces.

Grant Hirabayashi, Roy Matsumoto and Tom Tsubota were among the 14 MIS men assigned to Merrill's Marauders in Burma. There, Matsumoto crawled within feet of the enemy to overhear plans of an attack. Alerting his unit, he saved it from annihilation.

Tom Sakamoto was one of three linguists to serve at the Japanese surrender ceremony aboard the USS Missouri in September 1945. He stayed in the Army after the war and retired as a colonel, as did Harry Fukuhara. Sakakida, Matsumoto, Fukuhara and Harry Akune, who served in the Philippines, are among several MIS veterans in the Military Intelligence Hall of Fame. But most World War II Nisei linguists, in spite of their important role in the war effort, never advanced beyond technical sergeant, owing to the double standard in place at the time.

After Japan's surrender, the American occupation forces needed more linguists than ever. The entire country had to be rebuilt and its people fed. POWs returning from China, Manchuria and Russia were questioned for intelligence on our future Cold War enemies China and Russia. Subversive groups in Japan and Korea were surveilled and infiltrated.

The success of the Military Intelligence Service taught the American armed forces the importance of foreign language skills. The language school moved in 1946 to Monterey, California. Expanded and improved, the Defense Language Institute Foreign Language Center is one of the military's principal language training facilities. Several of its buildings are named for Nisei MISers.

Unlike other soldiers, MIS men did not serve in a single unit. Due to the specialized nature of their work, small teams of linguists — often only one or two men — were assigned to larger combat units. They knew few of the other soldiers, some of whom were suspicious of Japanese faces in American uniforms. It could be lonely and dangerous work.

Because the MIS did not operate as a single unit, and mostly because of their secret work, the linguists have not received the recognition of other distinguished military units. The government did not even acknowledge the existence of the MIS until 1972, and it was not until April 3, 2000, that the MIS received its first commendation as a unit. President of the MIS Association, Marvin Uratsu accepted a Presidential Unit Citation for the Military Intelligence Service, the highest award a single unit can receive. Eleven years later, MIS veterans were each awarded the Congressional Gold Medal for their bravery and outstanding service during World War II.

Roy Matsumoto

"I was lucky. I don't need a medal."

Heroes may not actually disavow their courageous actions, but they often deflect them as acts of duty, impulse or luck. Roy Matsumoto is a fisherman, and fishermen understand luck.

Matsumoto's name is rarely spoken without one of the titles he so proudly deserves: Ranger, MIS Veteran, Master Sergeant or Merrill's Marauder. The 20-year Army veteran chose the quiet shore of San Juan Island to spend his retirement. On a calm morning, a dense fog obscured the view from his deck and dampened any sound, except for the occasional seabird and a single blast of an unseen foghorn. It seems as far as possible from the jungles of Burma and China, and the streets of war torn Japan.

These days Matsumoto stays active with the local Lions Club, and his newest project, collecting eyeglasses for the poor. But he is most recognized for his accomplishments during World War II, and for continuing to accumulate awards and medals. The walls of his modest home are covered with certificates, newspaper clippings and photographs. One recent photo shows the compact Matsumoto towered over by Army generals at Fort Benning.

"There are 13 stars there," among the five generals, Matsumoto pointed out. "And in the middle, there's 'Sgt. Snafu,' " he joked, pointing out himself.

An older photo showing Gen. Frank Merrill awarding Matsumoto a Legion of Merit hangs next to a framed commendation for a Bronze Star with Combat V for Valor, a medal for which Matsumoto waited 53 years.

Matsumoto volunteered for service from the internment camp at Jerome, Arkansas, and entered the Military Intelligence Service Language School in frigid Minnesota. Upon graduating, he took basic training along with the Nisei of the 442nd Regimental Combat Team at Camp Shelby, Mississippi. From Fort Mason in San Francisco, he sailed into the Pacific, finally arriving in India 40 days after leaving the Golden Gate.

He was assigned to an I&R, Intelligence and Reconnaissance, platoon of the 2nd Battalion of the 5307th Composite Unit (Provisional), jungle fighters led by Brig. Gen. Frank D. Merrill, and aptly nicknamed Merrill's Marauders. The Marauders entered Burma (now Myanmar) from the Indian border city Ledo, and fought commando actions in the Burmese jungle, where they battled tropical diseases and disrupted Japanese troops from their planned invasion of India.

In the jungle, Matsumoto discovered a communications wire running through the treetops. Borrowing a telephone handset from Lt. Philip Piazza (Piazza later founded the Merrill's Marauders Association), he scrambled up the tree and tapped the line, listening in on enemy communications. The dialect Matsumoto heard was unusual, but one he understood. Soon his position was discovered, and for the rest of the day he eavesdropped under enemy fire, bullets peppering his tree but not hitting him. He learned the location of the enemy's ammunition dump hidden in the jungle, which an American air attack quickly destroyed. Other intelligence he obtained allowed the Marauders to avoid previously unknown concentrations of enemy troops.

The siege of Nhpum Ga, began the 28th of March, 1944, during the Marauders' second campaign, thrust the 2nd Battalion into prolonged combat. The men found themselves out of water, low on supplies and surrounded by superior enemy forces.

"We had a water hole until they set up a machine gun over it," Matsumoto said. "Planes dropped water to us in plastic bags, but sometimes the bags burst." Throughout the 14-day ordeal, he said, "I could stand anything except the smell of the enemy dead."

One night toward the end of the siege, Matsumoto crawled within a few feet of the enemy, overhearing plans of a massed attack at dawn against a single American sector held by Lt. Edward McLogan's platoon. Forewarned, the Americans ambushed the first wave of attacking Japanese soldiers. The second wave began to retreat until Matsumoto stood and yelled the order to "Charge!" sending the remaining enemy troops to their destruction. No American soldiers were killed or wounded, but the enemy left 54 dead, including two officers.

Matsumoto was on track for the Medal of Honor until, he says, the 2nd Battalion commander, a Texas colonel, dismissed the award, saying, "He was only an enlisted man doing his duty. He's of Jap descent, and a Jap don't deserve it."

Having successfully blunted Japan's plans in Burma, Merrill's Marauders fulfilled its provisional mission and disbanded in August 1944. Only a handful of men had survived months of jungle combat without wounds or debilitating tropical diseases.

Over the last 65 years, the retired soldier and fisherman has had plenty of time to consider what happened at Nhpum Ga.

"I saved the 2nd Battalion, at least 800 men," Matsumoto said. "I was lucky. I don't need a medal. I could be dead."

Tom Sakamoto

"We faced three adversaries."

Retired Army Colonel Tom Sakamoto selected a familiar photo that showed him amid the crush of officers on the USS Missouri's deck at the Japanese surrender ceremony, and another of him with President Eisenhower. He studied the photos before handing them to his visitor. A few minutes passed before he softly began to speak.

"We faced three adversaries: the enemy, animosity in the ranks, and the segregation of Japanese Americans. The irony is, later in my life, I had Top Secret clearance and was in charge of military and civilian security for the 6th Army in eight western states."

Sakamoto was born in 1918 in San Jose, California, and spent four years in high school in Kumamoto, Japan.

He recalls, "I was well-versed with linguistics and the climate of war. Japan was chaotic, and I knew war with the U.S. was imminent. Even in 1938, I knew that. There were many Japanese Americans in our school in Kumamoto, and we talked how one day we may be fighting each other."

Sakamoto returned to California in time to be drafted, February 26, 1941. That summer, in the midst of maneuvers, he was approached by a man in civilian clothes, Kai Rasmussen, a West Point graduate and young Army captain, destined to lead the MIS Language School.

"He gave me a black book of military tactics from the 'West Point' of Japan. When I started to read it, his eyes opened wide. He asked, 'How would you like to attend a secret school and become an officer?'"

Sakamoto joked, "I was a buck private, covered in dust and surrounded by rattlesnakes. I wouldn't make lieutenant until 1945, but the choice was easy. I joined a class of 60, all Nisei except for two Caucasians. Only 35 of us graduated. I was sent to Camp Savage, Minnesota, to a broken-down men's homeless shelter as a language instructor. My folks were in a camp in Rohwer, Arkansas. One day I volunteered to go overseas, and soon, Gene Uratsu and I took 60 enlisted men to Brisbane, Australia."

Sent on to Finchaven, New Guinea, then southwest to Goodenough Island, in February 1944, Sakamoto met up with 1,000 soldiers, elements of the 1st Cavalry Division reconnaissance group, waiting to board nine destroyers. They were heading 400 miles north of Rabaul to take and hold a key airbase on Los Negros Island. The airbase and harbors on Los Negros made it a strategic point in the South Pacific.

Sakamoto remembers, "I was the only Nisei. I looked for a chapel and went to pray before I boarded a battleship and sailed at high speed overnight to the coast of Los Negros. We went down rope ladders under enemy machine gun fire. Brig. Gen. William Chase, the commanding officer, worried about my safety. When I took off my jacket in that tropical weather, I looked just like the enemy. Mike Garrity, a six-foot-tall New York cop, stayed with me the whole time, even to the toilet — we were that close."

During the operation, Sakamoto translated captured enemy plans revealing a planned midnight counterattack.

"I hurriedly translated for the general. The rain made the pages stick together, so I couldn't even go back over it. I learned Baba, the Japanese battalion commander, was to lead the attack. Gen. Chase called in fire from our nine destroyers."

The enemy commander, Baba, was killed in the bombardment and the attack blunted, but survivors planned their own suicidal *banzai* charge.

"We saw movement in the grass 50 yards away, and I went forward to get them to surrender," Sakamoto said. "I shouted, 'You are surrounded. Your defeat is certain. Please surrender.' Instead, they threw a hand grenade at us."

His humane calls for surrender failed, but the Americans prevailed and Sakamoto was awarded a Bronze Star for his impromptu translation of the enemy orders. He would later earn a second Bronze Star in Korea and a Legion of Merit for service in Vietnam. But greater than the medals is his pride of his military service and the high-level assignments he completed, including his work at the surrender ceremony aboard the Missouri. He was also the first Nisei to visit Hiroshima after the bombing, accompanying a group of journalists.

"On the way, the press was excited, saying, 'This is the story of the century.' When we got to the Red Cross Hospital it was full of bodies. Not soldiers, but women, old men and children, their skin burned off. The press took one look and recoiled. On the way back, no one spoke. Their enthusiasm was gone."

He took a deep breath.

"Loyalty is something, no matter how fluent you speak it or write it, it has to be demonstrated in the end. History supports the betterment of our society, and I hope and pray we did some good for our country. Despite the adversity we faced, we were proud to serve our country."

Fred Kitajima

"If the Emperor didn't surrender, we would still be fighting over there."

Kitao Kitajima was the eldest son, followed by Fred, Robert, Katsumi and Takanobu — five brothers separated by oceans, fate and divided allegiances. Their common hope: not to face each other in battle.

Years later, Fred Kitajima, a Military Intelligence Service veteran, looked back on the war and shared his family's story from a kitchen chair sitting next to his wife, Dorothy.

Drafted in February 1941, months before the war started, Fred remembers the Army discharging many Nisei soldiers in 1942. And he remembers his brother, Kitao, losing his grocery business and new house when he and his family were interned. Kitao's wife gave birth to their son, Dickey, while imprisoned at the Bay Meadows Assembly Center, a converted horserace track near San Francisco, before being sent to the Topaz War Relocation Center in Utah.

Fred and Robert both studied in separate classes at the MIS Language School at Camp Savage, Minnesota. Fred's barracks were all men from Hawaii who, unlike him, never went through basic training, but had been sent directly to language school. Fred completed the six-month program, then advanced training, at nearby Fort Snelling. Robert shipped out, and the brothers lost track of each other for the rest of the war.

Fred later learned Robert flew missions from Guam, dropping propaganda leaflets over Japan, where some fluttered toward the city of Fukuoka to be caught by their youngest brother, Takanobu. Their brother Katsumi had been drafted into the Japanese army and stationed on an island between Japan and Korea. Fred ended up in northern Luzon aiding the Filipino guerrillas. "I interrogated prisoners, so was not in the middle of combat," he said. "But I could hear the American bombing 24 hours a day. By then, Japanese POWs were all young soldiers who felt there was no reason to keep fighting, a different attitude from earlier in the war."

When the war ended, Fred sailed through a typhoon to Quonju (Gwangju), Korea, where communists were gaining a presence in the power vacuum left by the departing Japanese. Communists beat the block leaders bloody, fought in the streets and incited riots in front of the provisional capitol. Fred said he was there in the middle of the crowd, listening for intelligence.

During the decades-long Japanese occupation of the country, educated Koreans were taught Japanese. Civilian and government leaders all spoke the language, providing endless work for Fred. The only American linguist in Quonju, he worked long hours enduring the typhoon rains and mud, carrying a weapon for his own defense. He interrogated communist leaders and interpreted in court, and for the police, finance and transportation departments.

"It was rough," Fred said. "I used my helmet to wash my face and brush my teeth. There was no mess hall to eat in, just a field kitchen to warm up K-rations, Spam and stew. You could not eat Korean food because they used human fertilizer. But we bought 10 fresh eggs for $3.00 and boiled them on top of the potbelly stove."

As in the Philippines, Fred observed, American soldiers happily passed their meal scraps to the desperate civilians. Korean and Filipino civilians shared a common poverty, all victims of war and their countries' grossly inequitable divisions of wealth.

By Christmas 1945, Fred joined thousands of GIs sailing home from Korea. The 90-year-old lights up like a kid on Christmas morning, eyes smiling and a grin stretching from ear to ear as he relives the happy memory of that day, as Dorothy looks on quietly, smiling proudly at her husband.

"Those Navy guys had a feast prepared with turkey, stuffing, fresh vegetables, everything you can imagine. A real Christmas Dinner!" he beamed.

He helped himself to the first real food in months, appreciative of the warm Navy hospitality and knowing he was among friends and on his way home to family.

His brother Robert was one of only a few MIS men to serve in the Army Air Corps during the war. He set the marker for the Hiroshima atomic bomb, and surveyed A-bomb effects, entering Hiroshima five days after the bombing and Nagasaki three days afterward. Robert eschewed veterans' organizations, keeping tight-lipped about his missions, what he did and what he saw. He never shared his experiences with Fred.

Their family had many relatives in Japan during the war. For their sake and his own, Fred is able to justify the atomic bomb.

"There is an old saying, *yamatodamshi* — 'dedicated to the Emperor.' Those with the old way of thinking — they would never give up — they would fight to the end," he explained.

"If the Emperor didn't surrender, we would still be fighting over there."

Nobuo D. Kishiue

"I'll shoot you right back!"

The folks around Fresno must share a good sense of humor, at least those who named the area's towns. Along with Clotho, Raisin City, Parlier and Dinuba, places with names like Ivanhoe, Big Bunch, Uva, Lacjac and Armona mark the map.

Nobuo D. "Dick" Kishiue, an MIS veteran, was born here to a farming family in Armona and, in 1938, graduated from the high school over in Hanford, a bigger town five miles away. Until retirement, and except for his Army years, he toiled at the valley's fertile fields raising grapes and field crops — cotton and alfalfa — and, like some other farmers, he sprinkles his speech with the occasional cuss word. Upon meeting for the first time, he looks you in the eye and sizes you up before gripping your hand. Kishiue told his story one evening in his VFW post's meeting room in a historic building on Hanford's iconic town square.

Kishiue was drafted in September 1941 and sent west across the San Joaquin Valley for 16 weeks' basic training at Camp Roberts. Following the attack on Pearl Harbor, he found himself transferred to Camp Robinson, Arkansas. Within months, his parents, two sisters and younger brother were uprooted and also sent to Arkansas, but to the Jerome War Relocation Center.

"At basic training, an Army officer came around Camp Roberts and asked me about reading Japanese," Kishiue said. "Another officer came around again at Camp Robinson, and by December 1941, I was in the second class of the Japanese language school at Camp Savage, Minnesota. When we graduated six months later, 10 of us were sent to Hawaii and attached to the 27th Infantry Division."

In Hawaii, the 10 new MIS men were split up, with Kishiue and his friend Jack Tanimoto assigned to the 165th Infantry Regiment's 2nd Battalion.

"My buddy Jack was four years older than me and could read *kanji* (Japanese characters) better. We worked as a team."

That two-man team of linguists served an entire battalion.

"Our regiment attacked Makin in the Gilbert Islands the same time the Marines hit Tarawa, that's why nobody heard about Makin. When we hit Makin, I found some papers and discovered we were facing a company of Imperial Marines of the Japanese Navy — they were tough, six-foot guys, a select bunch. But they were only one company and we had two battalions. I talked to the G-2 colonel, and he pushed our troops forward."

On Makin, Kishiue and Jack ventured onto a beach to examine an abandoned Japanese cannon, and encountered American soldiers shocked by their Asian faces in Army uniforms.

"We almost shot you," exclaimed one man, still shaking.

"Hell!" Kishiue said. "I'll shoot you right back!"

On the next island, Saipan, the Americans faced 27,000 enemy soldiers, and the fighting went on for three weeks. Kishiue, Tanimoto and the 27th Division advanced between the Marine 2nd and 4th Divisions. The Army troops encountered strong resistance, and their front line fell behind the Marines on both flanks.

"There were two General Smiths," Kishiue explained, "Army Maj. Gen. Ralph C. Smith and the Marine Corps' 'Howling Mad' [Holland M.] Smith. Our General Smith wasn't convinced the enemy was neutralized, and he wanted a 24-hour naval bombardment before we advanced."

A feud erupted between the two services, and Maj. Gen. Ralph C. Smith was relieved of his command. He would not advance without artillery — he valued his men too much, and they him.

"We loved our general," Kishiue recalls.

After a month in New Hebrides, the linguists boarded a ship to Okinawa, where Kamikaze pilots attacked U.S. Navy ships every day for 90 days.

"I saw them hit one of our ships," Kishiue said. "And I interviewed a kamikaze pilot who had ditched between two destroyers. I asked him why he ditched instead of hitting one of the destroyers, and he said, 'I had a 500-pound bomb under my seat and only enough gas for a one-way trip.'"

The pilot had decided to ditch in the ocean and live on, saving himself — and many American lives as well.

Kishiue continued, "For two weeks, we registered Okinawan civilians and fishermen, and questioned them about Japan's beaches [in advance of the planned American amphibious landing]. Then they dropped the bomb. It was good, but it was a sad day," he said.

With the war's end, the 27th Division sailed to Japan, where the Army needed MIS linguists more than ever. But after two months in Japan, Kishiue was ready to go home.

"I told them no! For the whole war I was engaged to be married and I had someone waiting for me at home. I went through the whole war as just a Specialist, and then they offered me a Second Lieutenancy to stay another year. Goddamn!"

Masaji Gene Uratsu

"We are talking about American Citizens, but with Japanese names and Japanese features."

The Army's first Japanese Language course was established at the Presidio of San Francisco just months before the U.S. entered World War II. Masaji Gene Uratsu was one of 60 original students. Uratsu and his three brothers all served in the U.S. Army during wartime, and a sister served as a civilian nurse during World War II. Uratsu retired from the Army after 21 years with the rank of Major. Even at age 92, with the war long behind him, he bristled at the suggestion of wartime disloyalty among Japanese Americans.

"Our loyalty was questioned by the military despite the fact that we Nisei were born, schooled and raised in the United States. We are talking about American Citizens, but with Japanese names and Japanese features.

"A Presidio graduate was in New Guinea interrogating a POW at the front line. A Caucasian captain comes by and says, 'What are you doing? You're a goddamn fool! Why are you even here when your family is locked up?' The guy looks up and says, 'Sir, I'm just doing my job.' *That's* what we did, our job. *That's* our battle cry!

"When the war started, we didn't know what was going to happen. I was already in the Army studying Japanese. Our Nisei friends, stationed along the West Coast, were discharged without cause and declared 4-C, 'enemy aliens not desired for the armed services.' Others stayed in the Army, but their weapons were taken away and they were ordered to wash dishes and pick up trash and cigarette butts. We were in the darkness, not knowing what our future would be. I asked an officer, 'Colonel, what's going to happen to us?' He said, 'If I knew that, I'd be working in the War Department.'

"Back then, we had 40 acres of orchard in Placer County, California. In my absence, my younger brother, Rusty, was in charge of running the farm. Rusty had the foresight to ask his agriculture teacher, Mr. Richardson, to look after the farm and keep the profit after the taxes were paid. Mr. Richardson was very honest, and as an agriculture guy, he knew how to take care of the fruit trees. My parents were away for four years, first to Tule Lake, California, then to Amache in Colorado. After they got out of the concentration camps — that's what President Truman called them, so I'll use that term — our farm was in the best shape ever."

Upon graduation, 30 linguists were sent to Alaska and the South Pacific; the rest to Camp Savage, Minnesota, where Uratsu, Tom Sakamoto, and eight others became enlisted instructors. Uratsu and Sakamoto volunteered to go overseas and, within weeks, sailed for Brisbane, Australia.

Uratsu recalled, "The chief at Brisbane wanted me as his right-hand man, but I volunteered to go to New Guinea. I said I have to go — I have students there. I got to New Guinea after the fighting at Buna and Gona. Originally, I was assigned to the 163rd Regimental Combat Team, then I was with the 'Bushmasters,' the 158th Regimental Combat Team. I made five amphibious landings in New Guinea and the Philippines.

"I didn't know Marvin was in the MIS. As soon as he graduated high school, he volunteered and joined an MIS unit in Manila. At that time, I was fighting in the jungles of Bicol Peninsula in southern Luzon. When Marvin went for his interview at ATIS (Allied Translator and Interpreter Section) they told him, 'Since your older brother is still fighting in the jungle, we will give you a less dangerous job,' and they assigned him to an engineering outfit. Someone tipped me off he was in the MIS, but I didn't see him until we met in Japan after the war."

Uratsu spent eight years in Japan during his three tours.

"Tokyo was devastated from the fiendishly accurate aerial bombings. My most important job was liaison with J2 — the new Japanese forces for the defense of Japan — Far East Command HQ. I'd deliver letters to the prime minister, the foreign office, the prefectural governor. I listened to what they were saying and passed it on to the intelligence chief. I was also responsible for the interpreting office of J2.

"We were told by the commanders, almost every day, 'You cannot discuss what you are doing with outsiders. It's classified.' So we were not comfortable talking about it, even when we were finally allowed to, even with our wife and kids," Uratsu said.

"In a way, the warning to safeguard classified information went too far, as many MISers went to the grave refusing to talk about their contributions. It's good the historians are now asking about our story. I'm 92. When we are gone, this information will be six feet under."

Takashi Matsui

"My brother was conscripted into the Japanese Army, sent to New Guinea, and never came back."

On a bright Seattle day, Takashi Matsui began the morning's lesson.

"When you are at war, you want to know about the enemy, his history and culture. Way back in 1941, there were only a handful of Americans who knew anything about Japan. The War Department had to rely on Japanese Americans."

At 92, the U.S. Army Military Intelligence Service veteran looked back to the war years, and farther — nearly a century — sharing history and the series of events that led his family's two countries to war. He spoke with authority and precision, signs of a good teacher. The creases on his trousers were knife-sharp, his black shoes shined and his fingernails flawlessly trimmed.

"I was born in Oregon. My mother took me to Japan and left me there with my grandparents. I grew up there in Fukuoka Prefecture, graduated high school and returned to Seattle. The economy was terrible in Japan — as bad or worse than the U.S. My father thought I would have a better chance in Seattle," Matsui said.

"I couldn't speak a word of English, and I thought, I better learn the language first. I enrolled in the Soho Foreigners School. Two Norwegian boys were in the class — funny, because I thought all white people spoke English! I went to Broadway High School, finished in 1938, and started at the University of Washington. I never finished — I was drafted in March 1942. I have a younger brother and two sisters, born in Seattle. They went to Japan and never returned to the U.S." He paused. "My brother was conscripted into the Japanese Army, sent to New Guinea, and never came back.

"Tojo *had* to go to war," the former teacher explained. "Russians had started to come into China, looking for concessions and a warm water port. This was a direct conflict with Japan. The Japanese fought the Russian army here and there — although the history books don't say so. The U.S. demanded Japan pull out of their war in China," leading to Japan's reaction, Pearl Harbor, and the history we know too well.

"When the Relocation started in May, I was in basic training in Arkansas. Many Japanese Americans were being discharged. Instead, I was sent to Fort Warren, Wyoming — to do nothing. We were told to move all the coal stoves to one corner of the warehouse, the next week we'd move them back. One day I was called by the company commander and told I was assigned to so-called Camp Savage, Minnesota. I was the only one to go."

The Minnesotans welcomed the Nisei, and the soldiers enjoyed themselves at the Chinese restaurants they found in Minneapolis. How about the winters?

"Terrible!" Matsui said. "The snow came in November and stayed there until April. Faculty lived in constructed buildings, but the students lived in tents. I stayed on as an instructor. The school moved in 1944 to better facilities at Fort Snelling, closer to St. Paul, Minnesota. I got married in 1945. She was from San Francisco, Mitsue Kono. We went to her parents' relocation camp in Utah to be married. For a honeymoon, we drove around the block.

"Classes kept going after the war ended. The school moved to the Presidio of Monterey in 1946. I volunteered to go overseas and was sent to MacArthur's headquarters, and after two and a half months, I was assigned to military intelligence. We processed Japanese military personnel coming back from the Russian military area, looking for intelligence on the Russian army."

In 1947, Matsui became a civilian worker for the War Crimes Trials. He said A-Class trials were for high-ranking policy makers, like Tojo.

"B-Class crimes included the mistreatment of B-29 flyers, denying medical supplies to prisoners, that sort of thing. The prosecution had months to prepare their cases. After they presented papers with the charges, we investigated for the defense. We had to prepare affidavits, interview witnesses. The trials ended in 1950. We were taking golf lessons at the Yokohama Country Club when the Korean War broke out. I thought they would recall me. They didn't." He smiled.

While teaching at the language school, "Some of the students wrote to me from the front line about the conditions, what they went through, what a rough time they had and how they succeeded. They sent tips on how to conduct interrogations, how to speak to officers, what not to say."

Would that make Matsui a favorite teacher, to have received so many letters? A former Language School student walked in and overheard that last question.

"He was tough," was all the student said.

Arthur Yorozu

"I was born in Seattle and interned at Minidoka."

Arthur Yorozu, one of the last soldiers to study at the Military Intelligence Service Language School at Fort Snelling, Minnesota, entered the U.S. Army in August 1945, a few days after Japan surrendered.

"I am one of six children; I am the youngest. I was born in Seattle and interned at Minidoka," Yorozu began his story, speaking with the efficiency of the engineer he was, referencing the Idaho prison that interned Seattle's Japanese Americans during World War II.

Once he graduated from the big high school at the Minidoka War Relocation Center, "Art" was allowed to leave for further schooling, traveling east for college.

"I was living in New Haven when I was drafted. The war in Europe had ended, but the draft quota went way up. Fort Devens, Massachusetts, was the first place I saw separate lines for 'Whites and Coloreds,'" New England then sharing one of the hallmarks of the segregated South.

Yorozu traveled to Camp Croft, South Carolina, for basic training, learning his older brother, Henry, was training there at the same time.

"An officer came around with a Japanese newspaper, recruiting for the language school. 'Can you read this?' I told him I could tell which way is up, but I can't read it. 'Was I interested in language school?' No! I had already been accepted to the ASTP, Army Specialized Training Program class at Yale University. So, two weeks later I was sent to language school at Fort Snelling, Minnesota!"

Henry joined his brother at language school, but Art says Henry was not very gung ho for the MIS. "He never took the language course. Instead, because he had some teaching experience at Yale, Henry ended up teaching chemical warfare.

"School was intensive, but I was determined to learn Japanese. Tak Matsui, the division head, was very tough, and would come in to check on us during the compulsory study periods. I was sent to Japan in September 1946. By then, the language school had moved to Monterey, California."

Yorozu worked in the translation section, handling documents used in the prosecution of war crimes. He described intense work, full of deadlines, and his front row seat on the reconstruction of Japan.

"I was the youngest kid there, 19. The next was 24. Tokyo was a mess. There was a food shortage, the railroad station and the post office had been bombed, and the rebuilding was so fast, I thought. We had some university kids working for us, and eventually they all asked about the justification for the A-bomb.

"In January 1947, I was assigned to interrogate Japanese prisoners from Manchuria and Russia. Most of them were sick. After the war the Russians dismantled factories in Manchuria and sent everything to Russia. If you happened to work there, you went too. A malnourished woman with two kids came through from Manchuria. I heard her speaking perfect English — she went to Cleveland High School in Seattle and knew my brother Bill. Her husband had been an engineering student in Seattle but couldn't get a job — they weren't hiring Japanese engineers. He went to Japan looking for work, like a lot of engineers, and got drafted into the Japanese army. She didn't know where he was," Yorozu sighed before continuing.

"My mother had told me, 'Please go see your relatives in Japan.' I went to their address in Tokyo's Kanda district, and there was nothing there. The district had been flattened. I found them in the Nakano district. My younger cousin was ill with pleurisy. He had trained as a kamikaze pilot. He was only 16. I gave him food. He didn't appreciate it, but his father did. Today, my cousin and I are best of friends. We visit each other. I write him in English and he writes back in Japanese."

Yorozu left the Army, returned to Seattle and continued his studies at the University of Washington. Veterans on the GI Bill, many in their 30s, filled the classrooms, and Art found old Seattle friends at the Japanese Students Club. Upon graduation, he went to work at Boeing as an engineer.

In its own way, Seattle accepted minorities, but restrictions remained in the years after World War II, according to Yorozu.

"My brother had a hard time finding a house. Any place he could afford, they wouldn't sell to him. And where I'm living now, years ago there were covenants barring Asians, people of color and Jewish people. Now I live in the midst of three synagogues.

"I was at Boeing 38 years," he said. "In 1970, they canceled the Supersonic Transport program. I had worked on the SST for 13 years. Boeing cut its workforce from 107,000 to 37,000, and that's when they put up the big sign, 'The last one to leave Seattle, turn off the lights.'"

Grant Hirabayashi

"I've been baptized many times."

The years leading up to Grant Hirabayashi's service in the Military Intelligence Service could not have been stranger: recruited by two countries and imprisoned by one before fighting against the other.

This unlikely story began on a small farm near Tacoma, Washington. The Hirabayashi family grew lettuce, cauliflower, celery, carrots, berries and Chinese cabbage. Grant Hirabayashi was one of eight children. He was sent to study in Japan in 1932, at age 13. He preferred life on the farm to that in Japan, where the customs were strange.

"They were always taking off their shoes, and they drove on the wrong side of the road," he said.

He begged to come home. An agreement was reached: stay and study for two years, and then come home. The two years stretched to five. In the 1930s, as Japan fought China, Hirabayashi, like other young men studying in Japan, listened to the radio news, and each calculated his timely return to America. The time came for Hirabayashi when he graduated Japanese high school and left for his home in the U.S.

"When I returned, Kent High School accepted all my credits, and I graduated in one year. Then I received my draft notice three days after Japan attacked Pearl Harbor. But if you enlisted, you could choose your branch of service. I wanted a trade, aircraft mechanics. I wanted to join the Air Corps, so I enlisted.

"Shortly after war broke out, I was in Jefferson Barracks, Missouri, with about 25 other Nisei — under guard. We asked, 'What is this?' 'Protective custody,' they said. 'What's that?'

"We were getting very concerned. We heard West Coast Nisei were being discharged from the Army and classified 4-C. We were finally released after 40 days and lined up for new assignments. I made corporal and had my own room. I felt like an American again. In no time at all, I was at Camp Savage and I began a very intensive course of study."

Completing the six-month language training, Cpl. Hirabayashi requested a furlough to visit his family at Tule Lake Relocation Center, in California.

"I saw American soldiers, wearing the same uniform as me, with their machine guns pointing into the camp. I saw people deprived of their rights, their dignity and their comforts of home. Here I was, a free man in an American uniform, respecting the oath I took, and here are my brothers behind barbed wire. I was angry, in a sense. I was confused. I was crying inside."

Hirabayashi began the long trip back to his post in Minnesota, the train conductor politely tipping his hat in respect to the American soldier.

"I realized I was fighting on two fronts: an enemy overseas, and prejudice here at home," he said. "I volunteered. I thought if I fought, I could help them get out sooner."

Back in Minnesota, he soon got his opportunity.

"'Chief of Staff George C. Marshall, on behalf of the President, is asking for volunteers,' they told us. It would be a dangerous, hazardous mission."

The War Department estimated American casualties at 85 percent, he learned later.

A commando unit was forming up under Brig. Gen. Frank D. Merrill. Hirabayashi described the 5307 Composite Unit (Provisional) as a special force for jungle combat and long-range penetration behind enemy lines in Burma. Dubbed "Merrill's Marauders" by a war correspondent, the 5307th was to disrupt enemy operations threatening India and support Chinese allies fighting the Japanese. The unit of 2,997 men depended on their 14 MIS linguists to intercept enemy orders and tap telephone lines, and to translate maps, documents and diaries. Survival in the trackless jungle taxed men to their limits.

"It took us 10 hours to cut through a mile of jungle, through elephant grass full of leeches," he said, his crooked finger indicating their size. "We crossed the Irrawaddy River over 50 times. Enemy machine guns would hit the bamboo, and water would pour out — I've been baptized many times. I had amoebic dysentery, and malnutrition since I was allergic to K-rations. The doctor told me I was on my own."

And he carried another burden.

"I had not only relatives, but classmates in the Japanese army. Each night I prayed I would not have to face them in battle. After the war, I learned I had a cousin and classmates in Burma."

Of the many POWs he interrogated in the jungle, Hirabayashi remembered one Japanese officer above all others.

"He called me a traitor," Hirabayashi said.

"I told him, if we were to cut our wrists the same blood would flow, but you are a Japanese fighting for your land, and I am an American fighting for my country. Don't call me a traitor again! He called me a traitor again and asked me to shoot him and I told him, No! I wasn't going to waste a bullet."

Thomas Kiyoshi Tsubota

"At least they didn't shoot me on sight."

"We had three battalions, 3,000 men, the same size as the 442nd," said Thomas Tsubota, veteran of the famed Merrill's Marauders.

Officially, the 5307th Composite Unit (Provisional), the Marauders were a U.S. Army unit that fought behind enemy lines in Burma (now Myanmar) during World War II. Tsubota was one of the 14 Military Intelligence Service linguists assigned to the 5307th. The linguists' greatest danger in the midst of a jungle battle? Perhaps their Asian features and the chance of getting killed by their own men in the chaos of combat.

"At least they didn't shoot me on sight," he said. Then he allowed himself a smile. "I had an easy time. Life is the way you feel," he said.

At 95 years old, Tsubota had become a bit philosophical. He sat outside his Honolulu home and talked, oblivious to the trade winds shaking his plants and flowers and to the lizards scurrying by. He had survived five years in the Army, jungle combat and tropical diseases. He sprinkled his conversation with Hawaiian words, and once, with a song.

Tsubota was already in the Army at the time of Pearl Harbor, drafted six months before December 7th, and assigned to Co G, 298th Infantry Battalion at Schofield Barracks, guarding the Oahu shoreline. That Sunday morning, men thought the many planes were simply practicing, like so many others they had seen, until they spotted the red circles identifying them as Japanese.

"We captured a Japanese officer from a two-man mini-sub. The next day, the body of a second officer washed up," Tom remembers. He and other Hawaiian soldiers were sent to Camp McCoy, Wisconsin, at least in part, because of fears Japanese Americans might side with the enemy if Hawaii was invaded.

"At Camp McCoy, two officers came around to interview the Japanese American boys, and asked if I wanted to go to language school. 'No way,' I said. 'I'm going to Europe to fight Germans.' They said, 'You are going to language school whether you want to or not.'"

Tsubota's Japanese language skills were first rate.

"I had attended Waseda University for three years studying political science and economics, then to Meiji University for specialty economics. I was a dual citizen, so while I was there I could be drafted by Japan. They told me if I don't go to the army training maneuvers on Mount Fuji, I won't graduate. My mother said 'Come home,' and I didn't wait for my diploma,

I took the next to last ship out, and my dual citizenship with Japan was *pao*," he said, using Hawaiian slang for "finished."

"At the language school, an obese *haole*, a Caucasian private, graduated from the lower class as a major. I was one of the top three students in the higher graded class and was awarded 'Best Student' by the commandant in front of the graduating class, and I got nothing. I wanted to show I was better. So when they asked about a special mission and said it's less than 50-50 you will come back, I volunteered. We had to show how good and how patriotic we Japanese Americans were," Tom said, gazing at the swaying green bushes, reminded perhaps of a foreign land, long ago. "When I went to Burma, I thought maybe I will meet one of those soldiers I knew in Japan," he admitted.

"In Burma, everyone had dysentery and malaria. Once, my fever from malaria was so high I looked down to my pillow and all my hair was falling out. I developed a hernia, and they flew me out in a Piper Cub from a little field in the jungle. In the hospital, one soldier saw me and jumped up, yelling 'Jap! Jap! I'm going to kill him!' The nurse calmed him down, and said, 'He's a good American soldier — he's in Merrill's Marauders.' The next day that *haole* soldier came by and gave me a salute.

"A panel of doctors examined me and said, 'You've had enough, you're going back to America.'

"I think about the past. I think about the present, too. I think about the boys whose fathers are in Iraq, Afghanistan, serving in Kuwait, all these important places — mothers, too.

"You know that song, *God Bless My Daddy*?"

He then sang the whole song.

"It should be called, *God Bless My Daddy and God Bless America, My Country*.

"Life is, to me, complicated," Tom Tsubota sighed. "Things change and you hope they change for the better, but sometimes it goes the other way. I think about the present, and that makes me sad."

Marvin Uratsu

"We fought in World War II to make a better world!"

"I was only a junior in high school during evacuation," began Marvin Uratsu, using a gentle euphemism for the forced relocation of Japanese Americans during World War II. He spoke quietly with a calmness that comes with the perspective of age, wisdom and faith.

"We got shipped out to a camp in Colorado, Amache, an Indian name they call it. I was 17. I didn't want to graduate from a camp school, so I applied to a school in Des Moines, Iowa. I ended up living with Judge Allen, a municipal court judge, and his family. They all treated me well. They hosted many other Nisei kids.

"Just before I was to graduate, the Army reinstated the draft for Nisei. I enlisted in May 1944 and graduated high school in absentia. They read my name at graduation and said, 'In the service of the U.S. Armed Forces.'"

After basic training at Fort McClelland, Alabama, Uratsu attended the new language school at Fort Snelling, Minnesota, a streetcar ride away from the Twin Cities of Minneapolis and St. Paul.

"Gov. Harold Stassen of Minnesota was one of the few governors who welcomed the Nisei. On Sunday, we'd get a pass and take off into town for church service, and maybe lunch at a Chinese restaurant. People would come up to us after church, asking, 'Would you like to have lunch with us?' The hospitality of the people was just great.

"We had to get up when the bugle called. After breakfast, we'd march by platoon to class. We mostly learned Japanese military terms and tactics. We didn't spend much time on ordinary conversation — that's something that takes years to learn. By February 1945, they told us to pack up to ship overseas. That was a tough time for guys who had to leave wives or sweethearts behind."

His company boarded the SS Sea Runner, a liberty ship, in San Francisco Bay, and sailed into the Pacific as part of a large convoy. The men reached Kwajalein, then Manila.

"Manila Bay was strewn with Japanese ships that were sunk," Uratsu remembered. "I guess some of ours were in there, too. We walked into the Manila Hotel, looked up, and the sun was coming through the ceiling. It had been bombed."

The new men were assigned to the Allied Translator and Interpreter Section (ATIS), headquartered in tents at Manila's Santa Maria Racetrack.

"A guy interviewed me and said, 'Uratsu? Are you Gene Uratsu's kid brother?' Gene was in the thick of it on Mindanao."

Uratsu's squad of 14 men was assigned to work with the engineers in Manila and, after the war ended, in Tokyo.

"In Japan, their army had been in charge — army generals who never left Japan — not the navy admirals who had seen the world and had a greatly different perspective.

"The engineers' office in Tokyo was located right behind Gen. MacArthur's headquarters. You'd see a chauffeur-driven black Cadillac with American flags on the fenders, the famous hat and corncob pipe, and all these Japanese people taking pictures of him. MacArthur did a smart thing. He allowed the Emperor to keep his status, and he talked to the Japanese people through the Emperor."

Uratsu was discharged in May 1946, returning to help on the family farm in Loomis, California, during the busy summer season. His folks had already been released from camp and were growing peaches, pears and plums. In the fall, Uratsu bought a few new clothes for himself and entered University of California at Berkeley to study business. When he graduated in 1949, he found a job with American President Lines, stayed for 15 years and eventually ran the company's passenger service to Japan.

Another Uratsu boy, Rusty, was drafted and sent to Europe after the shooting war ended. The family appealed to the Red Cross for his early discharge so he could work the family farm, which he ran until he passed away in 1999. A younger brother, Tom, was "a private who ended up in Korea."

The long-secret Military Intelligence Service was finally declassified in the 1970s and, in 2000, awarded a Presidential Unit Citation for its performance during World War II. Army Chief of Staff Gen. Eric Shinseki presented the citation to Uratsu, then President of the MIS Association.

"Our perspective is not large enough," Uratsu observed. "How do we strive to end wars and conflict all over the world? How do you overcome all that? There were 6,000 guys in the MIS. We fought in World War II for what? To make a better world! I think we should leave the world a better place," he said. "I'm for peace."

He paused, and pondered.

"An old man can dream — maybe it's just a pipe dream."

Glen Seichi Arakaki

"My father was heartbroken when I was drafted."

It takes two years to harvest sugarcane. If there are tougher jobs, the list is a short one. Sugarcane requires attention at each stage of its growth: weeding, fertilizing, picking off the *opala*, the dead leaves. Much of this handwork can be done by children, and it was, not long ago, in Hawaii.

Contemplating an age of childhood labor and war saddens Glen Arakaki, whose family grew cane on 26 acres they leased from Hakalau Plantation Co. on the island of Hawaii. Arakaki grew up quickly, was drafted and served in the MIS in post-war Japan. There he interrogated repatriated Japanese POWs from Siberia, many of them victims of frostbite, missing fingers, ears and sometimes noses.

His father had emigrated from Okinawa to work on the sugar plantation; his mother was a "picture bride," arriving in Hawaii at age 18 or 19. Glen was born just a few years later. He had two older sisters and two brothers. Everyone went to Japanese school after English school, and everyone helped on the farm on weekends and summers, growing sugarcane they then sold back to the plantation.

"Farm workers were deferred from the Draft," he said. "So when the war started, my father told me, 'Stay near home or they are going to grab you.' My parents didn't say anything, but I could feel it — they wanted Japan to win the war. I stayed home, and things changed during the war. Marines came to Hilo and then to Parker Ranch at Waimea to train before going overseas. When we went in to Hilo, all the Marines and sailors seemed like foreigners to us."

The war ended, and Arakaki was no longer worried about the Draft. He left the plantation at the end of 1945, found work in Hilo as a stevedore and, as his father feared, received his draft notice within a month.

"My father was heartbroken when I was drafted. He expected me to take over — I was No. 1 son."

Arakaki reported to Schofield Barracks for basic training on January 10th, 1946.

"They gave us Japanese Americans a choice. If you knew a little Japanese language you could take a test and go to the Military Intelligence Service Language School on the Mainland, or you could go to the South Pacific," he remembers.

Arakaki chose the MISLS. He experienced the Minnesota snow in April at Fort Snelling, before the school moved to the Presidio of Monterey in California. On graduating, he was sent to General Headquarters, Tokyo, where new linguists received additional conversational training.

"On assignment with an American lawyer, I went to Sugamo Prison, where suspected war criminals were held, and took a deposition from a Japanese naval medical officer accused of not stopping the execution of an American flyer. He told us of what happened. He said he could not go against his superior officer without being killed or sent to slave labor. I don't know what happened to him," Arakaki said.

"For about a year, I worked at the port of Maizuru, and screened Japanese POWs coming from Russia. Every morning and night, we took a boat to work and back across a calm bay. The Japanese Naval Academy was located there at Maizuru. There was a brand new cruiser sitting there in the bay. It had never been to sea.

"Those days everything looked so dark. People with ragged clothes lived under the railroad tracks in Tokyo. We didn't see much of the world outside of work, and they warned us about eating the food, since the Japanese used 'night soil' for fertilizer. There was no sign of the civilians hating us. Instead, they showed respect to us Japanese American GIs, they were humble.

"I was discharged in March 1948, went back to school and studied engineering. I went to University of Hawaii, took the Professional Engineer exam, passed it and got my license. I was a civil engineer for the Honolulu Water Supply until I retired at my first chance, at age 55. Then I spent two years as a civilian employee with the Army Corps of Engineers in Korea, and two years in Okinawa."

Arakaki retired from the Corps of Engineers in 1991, only to begin consulting on a big golf course as Construction Manager, a project that took five years to complete.

"Then, finally I *retired*," he chuckled. "I have a son and daughter, four grandkids and two great-grandkids. And," he smiled, "I played a round of golf this morning.

"The men I served with in Japan were maybe 90 percent from Hawaii. One was my neighbor, Takeshi Kataoka. He passed away a few years ago. Of them all, I keep in touch with just one guy — he called me today."

Grant Ichikawa

"It was heartbreaking to see so many people left behind."

A veteran of three wars, silver-haired Grant Ichikawa began his story, like everything he does, with enthusiasm.

"Since 1960, I've lived in Fairfax County, Virginia — one of the richest, dynamic counties in the U.S.," he said proudly. "I'm the first Japanese American to live in Fairfax County, they say."

Although he has called Virginia home for many years, Ichikawa grew up on his family's farm in Fairfield, California, at that time a sleepy little town in a beautiful valley of fruit trees, especially in the bloom of springtime, Ichikawa said. His father immigrated just after 1900, returning to Japan to marry and bringing his new wife back with him to California. Grant was born in 1919.

"We had a very benevolent landlord who told my parents, 'Give your son an American name.' He put three names in a hat: Grant, Charlie and one other — I suspect Ulysses. My father couldn't spell and I grew up as 'Grand.' In school, a teacher looked it up and found my name was Grant. I still remember it. It had an effect on me.

"My one wish was to go to college, but it was way beyond our means. Fortunately, in those days, tuition was cheap, and I worked as a houseboy for room and board and graduated from UC Berkeley in 1941 with an accounting degree. But no one was hiring Japanese American accountants — they didn't trust us. I earned myself a degree, but no one would accept me, so I decided to become a farmer. Then the war started, and they picked us up.

"I had just leased my farm and bought all new equipment. My parents could not be citizens and, as enemy aliens, expected to be picked up. I was a loyal American — this didn't apply to me, I thought. Curfews started; we had to turn in our radios and, slowly, I became concerned. Then the fateful order to the train station: 'Bring only what you can carry.' The train took us to Turlock, where the fairground had turned into a barbed-wire camp. We shared a horse stall with another family. I can still remember, that was the lowest point in my life."

From the fairgrounds, the family was sent next to the Gila River War Relocation Center in Arizona. A team of Army recruiters came around looking for linguist candidates. Ichikawa admits he only read Japanese at a beginner's level, but he knew one of the recruiters, Jerry Shibata, who graduated in the same university class.

"The only way to prove my loyalty was to fight for my country," Ichikawa said. "We were the first Japanese American volunteers from the camps. When they said, 'You can join the Army,' my life changed! About 28 of us volunteered from Gila River. MIS leader Harry Fukuhara was one of them. Another guy, Dan Obata, said he had to sneak out of camp or he would have been beaten up.

"My younger brother Tomio joined with the next group, volunteering for the 442nd, but ended up going to the MIS. He was assigned to the 81st Division and saw action in Palau, Peleliu. He died about two years ago. My sister Ada volunteered to be an army nurse. She went to school in Minnesota, and as soon as she became a nurse, the war ended. My parents were proud of all of us.

"At language school at Fort Snelling, we all qualified as officers, but we were sworn in as privates. It was cold in Minnesota — November — and all we had was light desert clothing. They swore us in and gave us warm army clothing. That warmed us, but it also warmed us just knowing we were soldiers.

"I remember our first order: Go outside and pick up cigarette butts. We learned to obey. When we graduated, all the Caucasians became officers; we were made corporals — blatant discrimination. We figured it was expected, as we were still under suspicion."

Ichikawa's MIS class graduated in December 1943, and the men were quickly split up and sent overseas. He ended up in Brisbane, Australia, interviewing prisoners for strategic information about the Japanese homeland.

His section of 50 men moved to the Philippines in June 1945. They received direct officers' commissions to 2nd lieutenant and accepted the surrender of Japanese troops leaving the jungle.

"They were all hungry and disoriented. We told them, 'You are prisoners of war. You have no country anymore. Tell us everything, and we will treat you well.' They 'sang!'" he said. "I think they were happy Japan surrendered.

"We were sent to Japan, and I was assigned to a unit of physicists and scientists measuring the effects of the atomic bombs — it's a part of my life I don't want to remember. My thought was, was the bombing necessary? Later, I did a lot of research and found it was necessary, so I can live with it. Truman made the right decision. Otherwise, many American lives would be lost invading Kyushu."

Ichikawa returned to farming but was soon recalled for the Korean War.

"I trained with other young officers who had been in school or starting businesses, and they were all pissed off they had been recalled. We were in the "Korean Pipeline," and no one gets out of that pipeline. Many of them were killed. We were infantry officers, but I had no training in the infantry. They would have put me in charge of a group of men, and they would all be killed. Instead, I answered a request for linguists. I worked for the CIC (Counter Intelligence Corps) and then a unit controlled by the CIA. When it was time to be discharged, I told them I was leaving, but they made me an attractive offer I couldn't turn down."

Over the next few years, Ichikawa took assignments in Washington, D.C., and served two tours in Indonesia — interesting, he said, because politically, it was "the hottest time in that country." Two tours in Vietnam followed, from 1971 until the end of American involvement in 1975. He was one of the very last people to leave the American Embassy roof by helicopter. It is a chapter of history that still haunts him. Many civilians who had worked with the Americans were left to their own fates, and to the whims of the invading North Vietnamese.

"It was heartbreaking to see so many good people left behind — many went to prison for 10 or 20 years," he said. "I became so disgusted, I quit."

Once back in Virginia, Ichikawa turned his disgust into service, and did whatever he could to help Vietnamese friends who immigrated to the United States. Some even moved in with him and his family. He remembers bathing one newborn in the kitchen sink because the family did not have a bassinet. He bought a truck to deliver second-hand furniture to the newcomers' apartments, furniture he bought. He would not give up on his friends.

"I don't think the U.S. should have been in Vietnam in the first place," Grant Ichikawa said. "But once we were there, we should have stayed. Instead, we lost. That is no way to leave a country."

Al Nipkow   Military Intelligence Service   World War II

Walter Tanaka   Military Intelligence Service   World War II

Harry Fukuhara   Military Intelligence Service   WWII   Korea

Frank Inami   Military Intelligence Service   WWII   Korea

Robert Hayamizu   *Military Intelligence Service*   World War II

Paul T. Bannai   Military Intelligence Service   World War II

Ard Aven Kozono   Military Intelligence Service   World War II

War in Europe

From the beachheads to the end of the war, Americans fighting in Europe faced an enemy on the defensive. The Germans had been in France and Italy for five years, plenty of time to identify and man the best vantage points and most defensible positions. They constructed concrete fortifications, laid minefields, established fields of fire, camouflaged positions and planned their escape routes. Most significantly, they mapped the countryside and its landmarks; the beaches, fields, forests and mountain slopes became blueprints for their artillery. Marching down one French road, a young soldier spotted white paint on a tree.

"Isn't that nice," he thought out loud, "They paint the trees over here," not realizing he was admiring an aiming point for enemy artillery.

Most feared were German 88 mm cannon, what the GIs called, "88s." Lawson Sakai remembers an 88 gun hounding a single 442nd soldier across a field.

"They followed him as he ran, BOOM, BOOM, BOOM, and finally hit him in the heel."

In the Vosges, German artillerymen timed their shells to explode above the ground in air bursts and tree bursts that sent shrapnel straight down at the Nisei. There was no safe place unless the infantrymen had the time to dig through tangled roots and rocks and fashion crude shelters of dirt-covered tree limbs over their foxholes.

Where French battlefields were forest-covered mountains, battlefields in Italy were rocky mountains on which infantrymen often could not "dig in." They piled rocks to create scant cover, instead. Germans typically held the strategically superior high ground. From the hills around Cassino, German gunners could see all the way to the beach, veterans said.

The 100th Infantry Battalion, the original Nisei outfit from Hawaii, landed in Italy in September 1943, attached to Gen. Mark Clark's 5th Army. The 100th fought its way north to Cassino, where it took heavy casualties, before being withdrawn and reassigned to Anzio to await reinforcements before fighting north again to the outskirts of Rome. The Nisei were in position to take the city but were ordered to halt. Higher-ups determined this trophy should not go to a Japanese American unit, and other troops were accorded the honor. The Nisei kept fighting north, and then rested long enough to meet the 442nd soldiers, fresh from Camp Shelby.

The newly formed regimental combat team's first significant battle was at Hill 140. The 442nd was well-trained but untested. Mas Tsuda said they were inexperienced and naively confident.

"We found out the Germans were good soldiers ... and got our ass kicked."

The 100th Battalion helped out their new comrades, who had learned they still had much to learn.

The hard-fighting 442nd was pulled out of Italy and assigned to Operation Dragoon, the invasion of Southern France in August 1944, two months after the larger and more famous D-Day landings on Normandy Beach. The regiment's Anti-tank Company, which had been detached and trained in glider operations, made their own, costly insertion during Operation Dragoon. The rest of the regiment made an amphibious landing and moved toward its objective, farther north in the Vosges Mountains along France's border with Germany. The Vosges and its thick forests formed a natural barrier that had thwarted invading armies for centuries. For the Germans, it served as a defensive line to stop the steady Allied advance. East of the Vosges lay only the Rhine, then the German homeland. Hitler ordered his commanders on the border: No retreat, and no prisoners.

It was here the Nisei liberated Bruyères, a large village cradled by four hills the Americans designated A, B, C and D. The hills were enemy territory, and each had to be taken before the village could be liberated. Fighting continued through smaller villages, including Belmont and Biffontaine. Then orders arrived from 36th Division Headquarters: Move into the mountains east of Biffontaine and break through to elements of the 141st Regiment that had been cut off and surrounded by the enemy. "The Lost Battalion," newspapers back home called them.

This was a job other units from the division had attempted and failed. The Germans were once again on a mountaintop, hidden and dug in, the forest a calculated aiming grid for their artillery. Because of the German positions and the terrain, any advance would be frontal and uphill against a prepared and determined enemy — suicidal. Were the Nisei expendable or just the best men for the job?

"A little of both," believed infantryman Shig Kizuka.

The Nisei rescued the Lost Battalion after four days of nearly continuous combat and heavy casualties. Bearded men emerged one by one from their covered foxholes, staring into Asian faces under the familiar GI helmets, gratefully accepting cigarettes and rations offered by the Japanese Americans. Forward observer Erwin Blonder, assigned to the 141st, sent a final message before his radio batteries died:

"The 442nd is here. Tell them we love them."

The 141st included many soldiers from Texas, and the state legislature later declared the Nisei honorary Texans.

The 442nd had taken terrible casualties in the operation. One company, its officers dead or incapacitated, was commanded by a sergeant. The regiment was tragically and dangerously depleted, but there was no respite. The wounded were evacuated, but the regiment was ordered forward to the next hill, then the next. Rest and resupply were still days away.

The men were finally pulled back from the line, cleaned up and ordered to present themselves to the Division Commander, Maj. Gen. John E. Dahlquist, for his commendation on their performance. A smattering of exhausted soldiers stood before the general, looking like zombies, a skeleton of the full regiment he was expecting. Dahlquist demanded to know why the entire regiment was not present.

"The rest are dead or in the hospital," was the reply.

No longer a viable fighting force, what was left of the regiment was reassigned to the French-Italian border along the Mediterranean while it awaited reinforcements from Camp Shelby, and the 522nd Field Artillery Battalion was reassigned to the 45th Division, which advanced into Germany early in 1945. Italy capitulated and was out of the war, but German troops still occupied the country, right up to the French-Italian border. Germans and Americans laid minefields across the mountainous terrain. There was no fighting comparable to what they had experienced in the Vosges, but combat patrols, mines, mortars and casualties reminded everyone the war was still on. After a few months of the so-called "Champagne Campaign" and the arrival of reinforcements, Gen. Mark Clark ordered the 442nd back to Italy, and French troops took over their positions on the border.

Back to full strength, the 442nd was reinserted into the Italian battlefield at Livorno (or "Leghorn") and attached to the 92nd Division, a segregated unit of African American soldiers. They were back in the Italian mountains, this time against Germans occupying the Gothic Line, a final defensive line before the Po Valley and guarding the route to the Reich. Here the 442nd fought from mountain to mountain, as usual, always starting at the bottom.

Mount Folgorito was a formidable strongpoint and key to a portion of the defensive line. Before the arrival of the Nisei, months of attacks against the mountain had failed. One night men of the 442nd, led by Italian Partisans, hiked stealthily up narrow mountain trails in the dark, each soldier holding onto the man in front of him. They attacked the Germans from the rear shortly after daybreak. Taken by surprise, many surrendered at once. The fighting lasted only 32 minutes.

Combat continued in the Po Valley as the 442nd liberated villages and chased the Germans north, fighting in Italy until the end of the war.

The 522nd artillery had pushed into southern Germany. Outside Munich, they came upon the Dachau concentration camp — not a single camp, but a series of over 100 farms and sub-camps, they said. Officers warned the men of what they might find and ordered them not to give food to the captives, as solid food might be fatal to those suffering severe malnutrition. Sometimes they could not turn away the desperate prisoners, judging the poor souls would not survive in any event.

As the fighting ended, some soldiers headed home to the U.S. Others guarded German POWs in Leghorn, easy duty after combat. Some took courses in preparation for college studies back home. The war in Europe ended in May 1945, but the last 442nd soldiers would not sail home until April 1946.

Hideo "Pakala" Takahashi

"We called in artillery and it fell on our hill, instead."

Hideo Takahashi is a fisherman, never happier than when setting out from his hillside home to catch octopus and other delicacies. One afternoon he took time to sit on his shady porch and talk story about old Maui, once full of plantations and mills, and a young Pakala (his nickname since childhood), a soldier in the 442nd Regimental Combat Team.

Pakala grew up not far from his current home, on a plantation owned by Baldwin Packers. His parents worked there as share-croppers, planting and caring for pineapples until the harvest. At harvest time, they hired neighbors who picked the pineapple, loaded them into baskets strapped to their backs, then carried them out to the road where kids broke off the tops and packed them into boxes. That was then. Now the cannery is a shopping mall, the sole functioning cannery is in Wailuku, and the island has but one sugar mill.

Pakala's mother was Hawaii-born, from the island of Kauai; his father, from Japan. A photo of the Emperor hung on the wall at home. After Pearl Harbor, his father took the photo down, and Pakala never saw it again.

Governor Burns of Hawaii encouraged Japanese Americans to volunteer, thinking it would reduce discrimination and, especially, help the mainland Japanese Americans, many of whom had been interned. Pakala enlisted in March 1943 at age 18 and did not see his recent diploma from Lahainaluna High School until it caught up with him at Camp Shelby.

"Most of the original 442nd were from Hawaii, most of the replacements from the mainland," Pakala explained. "We were a regimental combat *team*, larger than a normal regiment. We had our own engineers, own artillery, own anti-tank and medical corps."

The 442nd landed in Naples and moved to Bagnolia, outside Naples, to a staging area, for about a month before going into action at Hill 140.

"We called in artillery and it fell on our hill, instead. Ko Ito lost his leg. We carried him down the valley and to a medical unit. He lived in Long Beach until he died. At our first reunion, he stepped on a bee on the beach. He was hopping all over, and I joked about it and told him you have to watch out for sand sharks!"

Pakala was wounded in the leg at Hill 140 and found a hole in his helmet the size of a quarter.

"My helmet was bent so much it would not go back on my head," a casualty of shrapnel from a German tank's 88 mm gun. He was wounded again in the Apennine Mountains and had a Silver Star pinned on him in a field in Italy.

With two Purple Hearts and a Silver Star, he was in the first group of 442nd soldiers sent back to the States at the end of the war in Europe. The whole regiment held a parade for the 77 men who began their happy but, in those days, complicated trip home. They flew on a B-17 from Naples to Dakar, Africa, then on to Brazil. From there, a small plane took them to Florida, stopping at little islands along the way. They rode in a Pullman train car across the country and were in Sacramento when they got word Japan surrendered. A few went into town and got drunk. They rode on to Oakland and then Seattle, where they boarded the aircraft carrier, Bunker Hill, which put in to San Francisco with engine problems before continuing on to Pearl Harbor. Pakala flew to Kahului and took a cab home to an empty house, missing his family, who were waiting for him at the airport. When they arrived home, he was asleep on the couch.

He went to work at the plantation, and "Old Man Fleming," the manager, offered him a half acre of land for $330 "because you were in the service." In 1947, he enlisted in a nine-month electrician crash course in Honolulu. He boarded at the church and worked part time at Sears Roebuck at night. He took a job with Island Electric Contractors for three years before working at Pearl Harbor for 29 years, the last four as electrical inspector.

His E Company was one of the largest contingents of 442nd veterans.

"We would get about 30 guys at the monthly meeting at the clubhouse in Honolulu," he said.

Pakala played softball at Ala Moana Park every Sunday in the 442nd League, pitching on the E Company team with Lefty Sugihara and winning seven championships, he said, until they started getting too old to play.

Barney F. Hajiro

"Maybe God saved me."

Barney Fushimi Hajiro sits a little taller than other residents of the spotless nursing home high above Honolulu. His shirt is pressed and perfectly white, with the 442nd insignia above his heart. Hajiro is energetic and impatient, and his legs pedal the wheelchair down the corridor at a surprising pace. Settling at a small table overlooking the city, he unfolds a sheet of paper on which he had carefully printed in neat capital letters his military decorations, the highest honors of the United States, France and the Great Britain. He points first to the listing at the top of the page, the one he is most proud of:

BARNEY F. HAJIRO
MEDAL OF HONOR
JUNE 2000
WHITE HOUSE
PRESIDENT CLINTON

Hajiro deserved the Medal of Honor, America's highest military award for bravery, in 1944, but during World War II, Japanese American soldiers routinely received lesser honors than their Caucasian counterparts.

"I guess there was some racism at that time...," he offered. He said little more about the medal, or his heroic deeds earning it in the Vosges Mountains, just west of the Rhine.

One of nine children, he grew up on the Hawaii Commercial and Sugar Co. plantation, the now the only sugar mill operating in Hawaii. Hajiro said old Hawaii was more accepting of minorities than other places, but had its own variety of discrimination based on the plantation system.

"My father, Shiroichi, came here in 1800-something when King Kalakaua wanted workers for the sugar plantation," Hajiro said. "Satsuyo Noda, my mother, was a 'picture bride.'

"Plantation life was tough. I would work 10 hours for a dollar. Cheap pay, eh? Compared to the plantation, servicemen got good pay and benefits, but there were no Hawaiians in the service — just white men."

He left the plantation full of optimism for a better life, but found few opportunities, even in Honolulu. He was living there on December 7th, the day America was thrust into war.

Hajiro knew many of the Hawaii Territorial Guard troops whose unit became the new 100th Infantry Battalion. After he was drafted, he met up with them again at Camp Shelby, Mississippi, where the 100th trained alongside him and the new 442nd. The 100th men were first to go overseas, and Barney wanted to join them.

"I saw them leave, but they wouldn't take me — I had no rifle training yet." He was assigned instead to M Company, a heavy weapons company.

Hajiro's voice was strong, with an occasional lilt from his Maui upbringing. As he spoke, he revealed his sense of fairness and an outsized measure of guts, even for a soldier in a famously gutsy unit. Rather than combat, he preferred talking about other fights in which his fists took the place of his Browning Automatic Rifle (B.A.R.).

"I was court-martialed two times," he said with a twinkle in his eye. "The first was at Shelby. I came in for chow and they told me it was too late. I argued with the sergeant — I won't say his name, but everyone knows who he was — and when two ranks fight, guess who always comes out on top at the court martial?"

In Italy, Hajiro came upon a 442nd soldier being beaten by a group of civilians. Seeing an unfair fight, he waded in, fists first. The Army docked his pay and reassigned him to I Company.

"I had many friends in M Company. I didn't know anyone in I Company, and I went into combat with no pay!"

It was soon afterward that Hajiro was awarded the Distinguished Service Cross for bravery during the fight to rescue the Lost Battalion. The Medal of Honor would not come for 56 years, but his scars have lasted even longer. He pushed up his sleeve to reveal a thin line running the length of his left arm.

"The bullet went in here and came out here. Maybe God saved me?" he wondered out loud. "After I was wounded, they asked if I wanted to go back to the United States. No! I said. Not as long as I have one hand to fight with."

Once the war was over, trouble found him again, this time in a Honolulu Chinese restaurant.

"A white guy — who was bigger than me — kicked me in the back and called me a 'sonofabitch Jap.' Why? He didn't even know me," Hajiro said. "We went outside and he went through the restaurant's plate glass window. The cops came but he was gone.

"At that time ...," he began again, perhaps remembering the America he fought for long ago. "I wonder if that man ever went to war?" he asked no one in particular.

Susumu Satow

"When I first saw a dead German, it really got to me."

The end of basic training left the 442nd's newest soldiers with a single question: What's next? One young private, Susumu "Sus" Satow, anxiously awaited news of his assignment. He finally got the word: H Company, heavy weapons.

"I became the last man at Camp Shelby assigned to H Company," said the World War II veteran and recipient of the Bronze Star.

Each of the 442nd's three infantry battalions was made up of three infantry companies and one heavy weapons company, the men who operated the formidable .30 caliber machine guns and 81 mm mortars. Just like the infantry companies, each heavy weapons company — D, H and M — was further divided into machine gun and mortar platoons, each commanded by a lieutenant. Six mortars made up a platoon.

Sus served in the observation post for one mortar platoon, laying the communications wire for their telephone link with the gun positions. Led by an officer or a sergeant, men in the observation post determined targets and called them in to the mortars. Sus said the high level of teamwork required for a properly functioning mortar platoon forged great friendships.

Mortars fire their rounds in high arcs against enemy troops, emplacements and vehicles. H Company's 81 mm mortars could hit targets nearly two miles away. In the rough terrain where the Nisei fought in Italy and France, the mortars served as portable artillery pieces because larger guns could not be moved through the mountains and heavy forests. The mortars' range was more than enough for close-in fighting, and the high arc could send shells over obstacles and onto targets conventional artillery could not hit.

Susumu, whose name means "move ahead" in Japanese, still lives in his hometown, Sacramento, California. It was there he met his future wife, Lily Higuchi, while both were students at Sacramento High School. The story of their interrupted romance sadly mirrored perhaps 10,000 other couples separated by the 1942 Internment when Lily's family was sent into confinement at Tule Lake, California, and Sus to Poston, Arizona, some 900 miles away.

"We were in a pretty tough situation in camp, that's the way I looked at it," Sus said, describing Interment with the same words veterans might use to describe combat. "Fortunately, the JACL (Japanese American Citizens League) proposed a Nisei combat unit be formed. It was, and I enlisted."

Once the decision was made to field Nisei troops, training at Camp Shelby quickly moved ahead, and by 1944, the new 442nd soldiers sailed to Italy to merge with the 100th Infantry Battalion. The men entered combat, and Sus learned he had no appetite for war.

"Lt. Gleicher and Lt. Stefnagle were both wounded by 88 shells as I watched, and it really got to me when I first saw a dead German," Sus recalled. "The first two Germans I saw dead — both of them young and blond — caused me to drop tears. I asked myself, 'Why does this have to happen?'"

Throughout the war, Sus wrote back and forth to his brothers and sisters, and, of course, to Lily. After the war, the two married in Chicago and lived there for a couple years before returning home to California. They were happy to find Sacramento's Japan-town "pretty intact," but having lived through the war, Sus had changed.

"We bought 20 acres, but I soon decided I would not make much money as a farmer," he said.

"At first, I didn't want anything to do with the military, but later, I got pretty involved."

He joined Sacramento's VFW Post 8589, the first Nisei VFW Post in California, served as its commander, and later as post chaplain for many years. He also accepted the higher position of VFW district commander.

Once he completed a four-year apprentice-training course at Sacramento's McClelland Air Force Base, he worked as a civilian on long-range and airborne radar projects for the Air Force. McClelland AFB closed, and Sus moved on to nearby Mather Air Force Base. Mather closed one or two years later. He concluded his civil service career at the Signal Corps Army Depot, which closed in 1995, then worked for a private contractor.

The oldest of four brothers, Sus was the only one to serve during World War II. Brother Bill served in the Air Force after the war; Oscar served in the Army during the occupation of Germany; and Leo, also an Army veteran, served in Japan during the Korean War.

Sus and Lily have two daughters and two sons. One son, Vernon, struggles daily with Agent Orange exposure he suffered while serving in the Army in Vietnam.

Roy Fujiwara

"The sniper knew exactly where I was... Pow!"

It seems Roy Fujiwara, a World War II veteran and lifelong resident of Seattle, will not slow down. He recently drove to Las Vegas and back for a reunion with his L Company buddies. He felt lucky to have made that trip, lucky to have survived the war. But he did not start out feeling lucky.

"I enlisted January 17th, right after Pearl Harbor, and I told my sister and brother, 'I'm going — I'm not coming back,'" he said.

In photos of the young men in uniform, it's easy to identify Fujiwara by his impish grin, one that stretches widely across his face. But describing the night assault on Mt. Folgorito, in Italy's Apennine Mountains, the grin disappeared and his sharp eyes found the focus they held during the battle — Fujiwara's last — peering at the enemy through the sights of his B.A.R.

The 442nd's last push in Italy meant assaulting the enemy's Gothic Line, a strategic series of defensive positions that had resisted Allied assaults. Italian Partisans led the soldiers up narrow mountain trails one night in order to surprise the enemy from the rear, in what turned out to be a quick and decisive victory. But any noise might have doomed both the men and the mission. Several soldiers fell from the trail that night, carrying their promises of silence to their deaths even as they plunged into oblivion.

"It was grim. No one was talking. The Germans could see everything — all the way to the coast. We snuck in there at night and prepared for the attack," he remembers. "A lot of the guys, when we got back, asked, 'How did we do it?'"

He went on to explain that at least one man in each infantry squad carried the powerful B.A.R., which functioned as a light machine gun.

"I was a big guy compared to the Hawaiians, and I was a B.A.R. man," Fujiwara said. "The B.A.R. weighed 21 pounds, and I could put it together with my eyes closed."

While his grin and sense of humor are big, Fujiwara is not a big fellow, so it is hard to imagine him as a young man, carrying his formidable automatic rifle and heavy ammunition up a mountain to meet a determined enemy.

"The Germans looked for us B.A.R. men first because we had the firepower. My buddy, B.A.R. man Joe Ochi, got shot, and I could hear him yell, 'Fujiwara! I'm hit!' I stuck up my head and the sniper knew exactly where I was ... Pow!"

The bullet hit Fujiwara next to his right eye and exited his neck, which today bears a six-inch scar. Not yet spent, the same round then shattered his right shoulder. His friend Ochi survived.

"War is cruel," he said.

"I could hear my squad leader tell the stretcher bearers, 'You better take Fujiwara down first. He's the worst — he may not make it.' It took us eight hours to get to the top, then all day to take me down. A jeep took me to a tent in a field where they did a hasty patch-up job. Then I spent 30 days in the general hospital in Naples. My bone was broken, and my jaw was wired shut. For 30 days, all I could eat was Jell-O and raw eggs. I owe my life to Ted Oye, another Seattle boy. He brought me down the mountain when I was wounded."

Fujiwara could not operate his jaw for a while, and it would take six months of physical therapy before he could raise his right arm. On leave from William Beaumont General Hospital in El Paso, Texas, he set out to visit his sisters, still stuck in internment camps. Although he arrived in uniform and wore his Purple Heart, the Crystal City, Texas, camp allowed him only a two-hour visit with his sister and her husband.

After the war, he returned to Seattle to find the Japanese American community trying to pick up the pieces of its pre-Internment existence.

"Most of the Issei from Seattle were farmers. In camp, many died, brokenhearted," Fujiwara recalled.

"I trained as a furrier, but I made one mistake: Seattle was not cold enough for fur coats! So I worked for Frederick and Nelson, the biggest and nicest department store there. They didn't hire Japanese Americans until I broke the color barrier. They hired me as temporary Christmas help — I stayed and I worked there for 32 years!"

Fujiwara absentmindedly ran his hand across the scar on his neck as another memory surfaced.

"You've heard of the *senninbari* — the belt with a thousand stitches? It's supposed to protect you, an amulet. My brother in H Company kept his in his helmet. I had mine around my waist. I don't know what happened to it. The doctors must have taken it off me when I was wounded. They probably didn't know what it was."

Roy Tsuya

"Don't be manini!"

Roy Tsuya grew up in Lihue on the island of Kauai. He had just turned 21 when he enlisted in the Army and joined the 442nd.

"I felt compelled to join," he said. "My father told me, 'Don't bring shame on the Tsuya family.'"

His mother cooked him a farewell dinner. When they said their goodbyes, it was the first time he ever hugged his parents.

"'Try to be a cook,' my mother told me, 'better chance you will return.'"

Roy rode a boat to Honolulu, where recruits were assembling to sail to Oakland, California. As they approached the Golden Gate Bridge, men came up on deck to see if the superstructure would clear the underside of the bridge. A train carried them through the Nevada desert, and it started to snow. The train stopped, and the Hawaiians jumped out to make snowballs.

Roy volunteered to cook on that train to Mississippi, and someone showed him the stove and canned goods and left him on his own. After basic training he attended Cooks and Bakers School.

"It was not much of a school," Roy said. "At meat cutting class they said, 'Cut it up,' and that was it! I almost went to MIS because I had Japanese school in Hawaii, but my friends started coming into the company and I decided to stay."

Roy and the Hawaiians found Camp Shelby and its tarpaper hutments awfully cold.

"We'd march in the morning with an inch of frost on the ground — crunch … crunch … crunch."

On a furlough to Salt Lake City, he met the woman who would be his wife and married her in nine days. Then he rode the train back to Shelby.

"In those days, you sat on the floor in the train. Every seat was taken. Everyone was traveling, soldiers on leave — going to see their parents. You'd sit on that floor all day. To go to the bathroom, you'd step over people."

His bride, Wuta, moved down to Shelby.

"The boys all came to our apartment when they got a pass," Roy said. "They didn't feel homesick since they had a place to come."

When the 442nd landed in Naples, he set up his kitchen tent and started cooking. By then he was a sergeant, with five men under him as well as eight KPs from the ranks who peeled potatoes and cleaned pots, and a baker who made doughnuts and other fare on a coal-fired stove. Roy served the men steak, roast chicken, fried chicken and rice. The vegetables and peaches came in one-gallon cans.

"The Hawaiian boys in line said, 'Don't be *manini*! Put some more!' Manini is the smallest fish in Hawaiian waters — with a small mouth. Everyone knew what that meant. Don't be cheap!

"The 'book' says you have to give men in combat one hot meal a day. In combat, the captain would say, 'Bring the food up.' At night, we couldn't use flashlights, and the captain's jeep and trailer would make too much noise, so we would each grab one handle of a pot — like a chain gang — and follow a soldier, up, uphill. They would whisper, 'No noise. No noise.' Even a canteen rattling was bad. Each squad leader would bring his men back for food for an hour or so," Roy said.

"A *paisano* showed up one day, didn't say a word, and started cleaning pots. He rode his bicycle home at night, and the next day he would ride after us as we advanced, and he would eventually catch up. We gave him food for his family. He replaced all the KPs. In Naples, people would come and take our garbage to eat. It was sad to see.

"I never fired a shot; still, I had bullets and shells go over me. Boys would come back from the front and talk with me about the fighting. We went overseas with 200 men and went down to 12. You never knew who was going to die."

But Roy would spend a year and three days in hospitals. His wife and his faith would sustain him through this trial and others. His brother James visited him in one hospital in Texas. James had been drafted and trained to fight in the jungle in Burma but was sent instead to the 442nd in time for occupation duty in Italy.

Roy attended college in Salt Lake City, worked for the Veterans Administration in occupational therapy and then worked in a travel agency until he retired at age 62. A Boy Scout leader for 12 years, he led many weeklong hikes and turned out over 50 Eagle Scouts.

On one hiking trip, a scout came up to the former company cook in the chow line. "I can't wait to go to Big Mac," he griped, and Roy didn't even mind.

Bill Omoto

"The Army, the war, it was an education — the whole thing!"

Sixty years after World War II, a reunion of 100th Battalion veterans still drew a couple hundred people. Most were family members, kids and grandkids; few were veterans. Of those, Bill Omoto was one of the young guys.

A retired accountant and city property assessor, William Omoto was born and raised in Monterey, California, and except for his Army years and his time in an internment camp, he has lived in the area his whole life. The home he shares with his wife, Margaret, is resplendent with treasures from their travels to Japan.

Omoto remembers Monterey as a community with great harmony between its people of varied backgrounds. Just 20 miles away, the town of Salinas was big enough to boast a Chinatown, with stores and foods coveted by Monterey's Chinese and Japanese families, and the Filipino fieldworkers who toiled in the region's rich vast farm fields.

His family moved a short distance to the town of Gonzales, where Omoto played on the high school basketball team. Within a couple of months, the attack on Pearl Harbor meant curfews and travel restrictions for everyone of Japanese ancestry. When Gonzales High School played nearby Pacific Grove, the team had to get permission from authorities in San Francisco for Omoto to travel the few miles to the game. Internment soon followed, with Japanese Americans losing their property, dignity and freedom. Early in the war, a National Guard unit from Salinas was captured in the Philippines, and its soldiers became casualties of the infamous Bataan Death March. As the news from Bataan spread, any bad feelings toward the Japanese, and the Japanese Americans in California, rose to an undisguised hatred.

"My father had just started his own business in Salinas. Bad timing — he lost it all," Omoto said. "We were sent to camp in Arizona when I was 16. They changed my draft status from 1-A to 4-C, 'enemy alien,' they said, and I didn't think I would ever be drafted."

His draft status changed back to 1-A in 1944; Omoto was promptly drafted into the Army, facing danger before he ever wore a uniform. Emotions ran high in the grim internment camps, where families divided over questions of patriotism and the loss of civil liberties. Draft protesters, called "No-No Boys," were apt to beat up anyone joining the Army. Draftees learned to quietly assemble after dark, say their goodbyes, and leave camp without fanfare.

"We had to keep a low profile. There were no parties," Omoto said. "One night I got on the bus to Fort Douglas, Utah, with another guy from my block, James Obata. We went on to Camp Blanding, Florida, for basic training."

Training complete, Omoto set off to visit his family, interned in Arizona. His train stopped somewhere in Louisiana. Nisei soldiers looking for the bathroom were met by signs: WHITE and COLORED.

Omoto remembers, "We stood around deciding which bathroom to use. We headed for one and a man stopped us, pointing to the White door. One of us said, 'We're not White, we're Colored.' The man said, 'You're not that color!'

"When I shipped overseas, I joined Charlie Company and met guys I knew from Watsonville, Salinas, Santa Cruz. The first question was always, 'What camp were you in?' The first guy I recognized was 1st Sgt. Louis "Royal" Manaka, from Monterey. He was in Service Company — that's where they parceled out new replacements to where they were needed."

Later, Omoto's squad leader was wounded in Italy's Apennine Mountains, and the man chose Omoto, the youngest soldier, to take over. A staff sergeant by the end of the war, he heard rumors corporals and sergeants would go home first.

"As it turned out, we went home last," he laughed.

"Our boat broke down in the Azores. After a week, we were running out of food and eventually down to one meal a day. Locals came around selling us bread and canned sardines. A boat sailed down from Bremerhaven to pick us up. We got to New York, but for some reason they wouldn't let us off the ship, and we were out of food again! After a lot of grumbling, they finally sent us to a mess hall. At the end of the chow line, a guy was trying to get people to 're-up,' re-enlist. Instead, the men were running past him! A couple guys from Hawaii actually did re-up because they didn't want to get home and go back to work in the fields."

Looking satisfied with his story, Omoto sat back and smiled.

"The Army, the war, it was an education — the whole thing!"

Masuo Tsuda

"Easy Company had a lot of heroes."

Their first two weeks in combat, the men of Easy Company took hill after hill without much of a fight as the Germans kept retreating across the Italian countryside. Things changed when they reached Hill 140 on July 4th, 1944.

"Hill 140, the first battle most of us saw blood," remembered Masuo Tsuda, one of the original 442nd soldiers and a member of E Company's 3rd Platoon. "We were green. All through training they brainwashed us. We thought we could lick our weight in wildcats, but we found out the Germans were good soldiers. We got overconfident and got our ass kicked."

Mas, as he is called, tells it like it is. He displays a certain seriousness, especially when he talks about combat. At other times, his eyes twinkle, and he is quick to smile and belly-laugh when reminded of the mischief young men seem to find.

Enemy artillery took its toll at Hill 140. The company commander was killed the first day of the battle. The tough little squad leader, Masao "Lefty" Sugihara, was wounded and replaced by Tsuneo Takemoto, who later earned the Distinguished Service Cross during the rescue of the Lost Battalion.

"Easy Company had a lot of heroes," Mas recalled.

The GIs learned to fear the German 88 mm cannon more than any other weapon. On the occasions when they were able to locate the 88s, U.S. artillery knocked them out — or at least made them interrupt their bombardment. More often, the enemy high-velocity shells seemed to find the infantrymen wherever they were on the battlefield, even in the dense forests of France, where visibility was only a few yards, or a few feet.

During one fierce artillery barrage, Mas peeked from his foxhole to see tall Col. James M. Hanley, the 2nd Battalion commander, standing nearby, looking for the 88s. Mas appreciated his courage and coolness.

Under fire, "The Colonel would roll a cigarette and not drop a stitch," he said.

The first week of October 1944, Mas landed in the hospital with severe frostbite. He no sooner removed his boots than the doctor returned with an order to send the walking wounded back to their units. Tsuda's frozen feet were too swollen to put his boots back on; they could not find bigger boots for him, and the doctors would not make him march barefoot in the snow. He spent the next two months in the hospital.

"It saved my life — I missed the Lost Battalion," he said, referring to the 442nd's bloodiest battle.

"I carried a Buddhist blessing with me all through combat. I still carry it," he said, leaning forward to pull out his wallet and the blessing, printed on a small card.

The card was in remarkably good condition, considering it spent months on muddy and rainy battlefields, then another 60 years in a back pocket.

"Some guys had the belts with a thousand stitches. We were all Buddhists, but they didn't have Buddhist chaplains," he explained. "So we would go to every church service they had — Catholic, Protestant, it didn't matter — we went to them all!"

Tsuda was a high school student when the relocation of Japanese Americans began in 1942.

"I was ready to drop out. Why bother finishing when they were just going to lock us up?"

He and his family were sent to the relocation camp in Poston, Arizona, where the internees cleared land and planted crops. Mas changed his mind about dropping out, and he earned his high school diploma at Poston. On hot days, he and his friends occasionally stole watermelons from the fields. Adults would chase them, and the teenagers threw melons into a canal which would carry the floating melons under the barbed wire and right into camp, where the boys waited for them.

After the war, Mas studied at night school on the GI Bill, became a landscape contractor and started his own landscaping company. His wife Ann worked in the office while he worked outside. His buddies from the 3rd Platoon were equally busy, and it was not until 1958 that they arranged their first reunion, held at Mas and Ann's home near San Francisco. Reunited, the friends made up for lost time.

"Ten minutes after they got to our house, we were out of beer," Mas chuckled. "We went to the store, and a half hour later we were out again."

George Oiye

"I was mad at the U.S. Army — the U.S. Government — for a long time."

George Oiye grew up in Trident, Montana, near the headwaters of the Missouri River. The town had a single industry, a Portland cement plant. Trident was far beyond the designated 400-mile-wide Pacific Coast relocation zone, and although Oiye had experienced little racial discrimination while growing up, that changed soon after Pearl Harbor, when his father was fired from the cement plant because he was Japanese.

Thirty miles down the road, Oiye was in his second year of aeronautical and mechanical engineering studies at Montana State University in Bozeman, captain of the ROTC Rifle Team and one of the few Japanese American students. Because Montana State was a land-grant university, ROTC was required of all male students. One day he was informed his draft classification changed to 4-C and he was not permitted to enlist, but still required to continue with the ROTC program.

On February 19th, 1943, President Roosevelt rescinded the Nisei's 4-C draft classification. With his background in aeronautics, Oiye set his sights on the Army Air Corps. Told that the Air Corps didn't want Japanese Americans, he petitioned the Adjutant General of the Air Corps Academy on his campus to allow him into the program. Following a lengthy application process, the general told Oiye he would make an exception for him. He joined up and, instead of the Air Corps, he was sent to basic training with the 442nd Regimental Combat Team at Camp Shelby, Mississippi.

"I was mad at the U.S. Army — the U.S. Government — for a long time," he said.

"I had never heard of the 442nd, and I had never seen so many Japanese Americans as at Camp Shelby. It was a sea of black-haired men! There were only 500 in all of Montana, and I had never seen more than five or six together at one time. I didn't know if they were going to send us back to Japan or what?"

Oiye was not happy about the blatant deception that sent him to the infantry, and not happy making just $16 a month. He requested assignment to the engineer company, but the company was full. His only other engineering opportunity was in the 522nd Field Artillery Battalion, the artillery arm of the combat team. He transferred to the 522nd, becoming the detail sergeant for the forward observer unit. The FO called in targets to a 522nd battery — C Battery, in Oiye's case — or, for long-range targets, bigger guns at division artillery, DIVARTY.

"You were not just calling up your own guns, but other units' 155s, or 'Long Toms,'" he explained. In fact, he called on an entire arsenal of firepower that included air support and naval gunfire.

He proudly recalled spying an enemy railroad gun secreted in a town on the French coast. The gun would only emerge from a rail tunnel long enough to shoot, but not long enough to be observed or attacked. Oiye searched for two days before he was able to pinpoint his target. He said "it was a clear, bright day" after several days of poor visibility as he watched two Navy cruisers fire on the gun and destroy it. He remained humble but seemed satisfied with the outcome and understandably proud of himself.

Oiye took many photographs during the war with his folding Kodak 620 camera and a "liberated" Kodak Retina. He published a book of his photos and experiences, *Charlie Battery: A Legend*, and he contributed photos and written material for other books and historical displays, including the Headwaters Heritage Museum in Three Forks, Montana, the Japanese American Museum of San Jose, California, and the Friends and Family of Nisei Veterans exhibit aboard the USS Hornet, docked in San Francisco Bay.

Following the heavy fighting in the Vosges Mountains, the 442nd retired to the French-Italian border for rest and reinforcements. In March 1945, while the infantry battalions prepared for their reinsertion in Italy, the 522nd was detached from the regiment and joined the American 7th Army's drive into Germany, headed for Munich. When the soldiers came upon Dachau's barbed wire fences and neat rows of barracks, they were stung with a sadness, and the irony of knowing their own families were incarcerated back in the States. Men from the 522nd have long said they shot the locks off the gates of the crematoria at Dachau's main camp, a fact historians would not confirm.

Oiye pored through thousands of photos, looking for one backing up the soldiers' claim. His tenacious work confirmed the 522nd's place in history as one of the units that liberated the infamous Dachau concentration camp. He traveled back to Germany to see for himself.

"Everything there was as the guys described," he said, satisfied.

John Sakamoto

"We always had plenty of rice."

John Sakamoto dependably presents himself wearing a Western-style bolo tie, cowboy boots and hat, and his shirt pockets will bulge with several long cigars. He is a craftsman, fisherman and musician, and he wants to live to be 100. He is nearly there.

He was born in Vernalis, California, a dot on the map consisting now of a single grocery store and abandoned train station. Out in the country, he drove a Model T Ford the first time at age nine. Sakamoto's father was from Hawaii and spoke both English and Japanese.

"He wanted to be an insurance broker, but he ended up a farmer," Sakamoto remembers.

One of his family's three boys and three girls, Sakamoto was drafted into the Army at age 21 — February 4, 1942 — shortly before the rest of his family left their strawberry farm and were interned at the Tule Lake Relocation Center.

"Nothing but rain," he says of basic training at Camp Robinson, a former National Guard base near Little Rock, Arkansas. But he remembers seeing Marlene Dietrich when she visited the troops, about the same time he learned of his family's imprisonment at Tule Lake. He wangled a 10-day leave and spent most of that time riding the train across the country and back to see them for a short visit.

For a while, he made $90 a month at Cooks and Bakers School at neighboring Camp Grant, the same good wage as a staff sergeant. But he was soon transferred on to Camp Blanding, Florida, for combat training, when Japanese Americans still trained with Caucasians, Sakamoto said.

"It was not until 1943, until FDR OK'd a Nisei unit, that we Nisei served together at Camp Shelby. Until then, Nisei in the Army were stationed at installations away from the coasts, usually in menial jobs."

Among the first replacements for the 442nd Regimental Combat Team, Sakamoto spent most of the war in the 2nd Battalion Service Company, which was responsible for the troops' mail, meals and supplies. He also played clarinet and saxophone in the regimental band. Among his photos, he keeps an old one of himself, cradling his saxophone and wearing his steel helmet.

Sakamoto recalls performing at the memorial service following the battle of the Lost Battalion, when the band stood stiffly in the snow for a long time while the names of those killed were read aloud.

"There were lots of names," he said.

His face lit up while remembering happier times — playing Glen Miller music in the ballroom of a big hotel in Nice, and his first plane ride aboard a C-47 from France to Italy.

Service company soldiers did not routinely carry weapons, but they had no doubt they were in a war. While holed up in a small town in France, they were shelled all night long and slept on the floor, curled under tables for protection. In Pisa, at war's end, the men were issued .45 pistols and guarded German POWs.

Always thin, Sakamoto had a good appetite and enjoyed Army food more than some soldiers.

"In Italy, we would trade potatoes for rice," he remembered. "We always had plenty of rice, and Spam."

He retired from the San Jose, California, school district and moved to the coast of Oregon, fishing and fashioning furniture and crafts from local woods. He lives now in Sacramento, in a small apartment displaying his military ribbons and many photos from the war years and later, from his time playing in the big bands popular at the time. Across the hall lives Helen, his older sister, and Sakamoto cooks for both of them.

At age 92, Sakamoto traveled to Washington, D.C. to accept his Congressional Gold Medal. He walked with a cane and with an extensive metal brace hidden under his trousers to support a bad knee. A group of active duty 442nd soldiers spotted him and rushed him with their cameras, as if he were a celebrity. They later posed together, with the World War II veteran in the middle and the young men and women crowded around him, all smiles.

Sakamoto has 18 great-grandchildren and two great-great-grandchildren. He says he is the only one of his siblings to never visit Japan.

Juno Kaneshige

"I'm no glory hunter."

Eighteen-year-old Juno Kaneshige joined the 442nd Regimental Combat Team in March 1943, and trained as a B.A.R. (Browning Automatic Rifle) man at Camp Shelby, Mississippi. He went overseas to become one of the regiment's first soldiers wounded in combat. His injuries sent him to the hospital for long periods and left him bitter about the experience.

The Kaneshige family — parents, four boys and two girls — lived on a sugar plantation on the Hawaiian island of Kauai. One brother worked in a sugar mill; another was a field worker. Starting at age 14, Juno worked summers on the plantation, sometimes paid only 50 cents a day. He was the only one of the four brothers to join the service. Leaving the Islands for the first time left him exhilarated, but unsettled.

"On the ship, you know you are going to fight the war, and I don't like it already. I'm no glory-hunter," he said.

In combat on Hill 140 in Italy, Juno saw a fellow soldier fatally wounded, his chest and shoulder ripped apart. Soon afterward, Juno was wounded in 13 places by a mortar round that also wounded his friend, Harry Yamaguchi. Medic J. J. Furuno bandaged him. "Tiger" Aoyagi and "Jumbo" Tagami crawled under fire to pull him out, amid "mortars falling, bullets flying."

Four men carried him over the hill to the aid station, then put him on a jeep to take him back, away from the front line.

"I think they all deserved a medal. I don't know if they ever wrote them up for one."

Juno spent four or five months in a hospital in Rome before being released to a replacement depot in Livorno, where the Army trained soldiers to fight again. A doctor eyed him skeptically when he arrived.

"The doctor said, 'What are you doing here? Let me see your X-rays.'"

Juno was sent straight to a hospital in Naples, and then put on a hospital ship to the States.

"The hospital ship was nice. You could smoke on the deck," he said. "You could wash every night in fresh water — while going over saltwater. The food was good. Breakfast in bed!" He laughed.

The ship put in at Norfolk, Virginia, and Juno flew aboard a C-47 to a big hospital in Palm Springs, California. It was nice, like Hawaii, he said. He endured four operations (the last two in Honolulu) and spent a total of 16 or 17 months in hospitals.

He visited his family on Kauai while on leave, but they never visited him in Honolulu.

"I didn't expect them," he explained. "The fare was $16."

Happy to escape plantation life, he went to beauty school on the GI Bill and moved to Chicago to work as a hairdresser for a dollar an hour. When it got cold, he moved back to Honolulu. He met his wife, Amy, a hairdresser at a shop where he worked briefly.

He took the civil service test for a U.S. government job.

"I got lucky," he said, grinning. "I passed."

He worked at Pearl Harbor, first as a timekeeper, then as an accountant, then for 26 years in supply at Hickham Air Field.

For years, Juno went back to Kauai twice a year to see his family and friends. The friends are all dead now.

"I'm lucky," he said. "I don't know why."

Mitsuo Honda

"I'm not really bitter, I just sound that way."

Mitsuo Honda sat in his comfortable living room in Pearl City, Hawaii, where the harbor's name forever changed the American lexicon. As a young man, 20 years old, he had been eager to join the service after the Japanese air attack. But he would have to wait.

"They wouldn't let us join after Pearl Harbor — that was galling! FDR is not one of my favorite people. He was like a white Brahmin, and it was nothing to treat us like animals. The only black people and Orientals he saw were probably cleaning the toilets." Honda snapped his fingers. "Like that! We were not citizens. But when they needed men ..." He snapped his fingers again and hung his head in disgust.

"We were real dead-end kids from the Depression. We volunteered in February, and we went in sometime in March '43. Most of the boys were from Wahiawa and Waialua, and we went together in our slippers and t-shirts to Draft Board 10, which was at our church. They said, 'Get on the truck,' and that was it — we couldn't go home. They sent us in total secrecy to the Mainland. We landed in San Francisco, but nobody saw us, and we were not allowed into town. I guess they were nervous on the West Coast.

"We were the 'original' 442. We got to Camp Shelby before the 100th arrived from Wisconsin. There at Shelby and along the Gulf Coast, they were sick of all the military people, who were everywhere, but they were happy to take our money," Honda remembered.

"There were always two water fountains, white and colored. They'd point to the white fountain and say, 'Use that one.' The last three or four rows of seats on the bus were for coloreds. But in Hawaii, we thought the back of the bus were the choice seats, and we'd sit back there. The bus driver stopped the bus, 'You, you, you, you. Move up here. Those seats are for the coloreds.'

"It took us 28 days from Newport News to Naples," he remembered. "War had been there for so long, the people of Naples were devastated. Ten-year-old kids were trying to sell their sisters who were just a couple years older. Kids would come into the mess halls with gallon cans, and you would scrape your tray into the can. The Italians were very nice, very warm, friendly people. We were the liberators, and we were chasing the Germans."

Combat changed for the Nisei when they reached northern France, and Honda's manner changed as he described the fierce fighting in the Vosges Mountains.

"France, it was very rough, so many of our boys were being killed. One time we saw a Jeep and trailer with one guy holding the head and the other the legs, and they'd throw the bodies into the trailer, stacking them up. It's demoralizing to see one of your men die. We saw dead Germans all the time — some were kids just growing up, maybe just 14 years old," he said.

"In Bruyères, it was all forest and it was so dark. I was a mine detector operator — I would sweep the roads. Fortunately, the Germans were in such a hurry to leave, I could see where they had planted the mines, and we would blow them up with a half a block of TNT. That made a crater this big," he said, stretching his arms out as far as they would go.

"I was wounded after 17 days — I got a little piece of shrapnel in the back. During the war, our engineering company had more casualties than the weapons companies.

"You don't hate the enemy — they are just doing their job, fighting for their country," he said and, as if offering an example, told of a neighbor his age, educated in Japan and conscripted into the Japanese army. "They brainwashed him, made him into a kamikaze and he died at Okinawa.

"Before the war, there was a beach for Army officers and their families at Haleiwa. We could go in the water — that is the law — but we were not allowed on the segregated beach or out on the officers' raft in the water," Honda recalled. "But we didn't really have discrimination in Hawaii, like they did on the West Coast. They were tough over there — but people went back after the war. I didn't understand that.

"The original 442 men are a minimum age 86 this year — I'm 89. I'm not really bitter, I just sound that way," he said. "But when it comes to race relations, I've seen it all."

Rikio Tsuda

"We moved toward Rome."

His friends call him Rick. Tall and lanky Rikio Tsuda served with the 100th Infantry Battalion during World War II.

"I was born way out in the sticks, at the base of the Koolau Mountain Range, in Takeyama Camp on a pineapple plantation. When the pineapple plantation closed, we moved to Haleiwa, and my father became a fisherman. Mostly he did night fishing from a 30-foot long sampan, and caught lobster and aji, small, shiny fish that are real good fried."

For a moment, a big smile filled Tsuda's long face. It faded as he continued.

"My father decided to give up fishing, and we moved to Honolulu. I had to drop out of high school to work as a carpenter's helper. Pearl Harbor day, I saw the bombing from where I lived on King Street. Several people were killed in downtown Honolulu from American anti-aircraft shells landing there. The American fighter planes sank some fishing boats — sank and killed some fishermen, too. When the night fishermen were coming home on the morning of Pearl Harbor, they didn't know anything was going on — U.S. planes strafed them and sank them."

He continued. "When the war started, we began building an airstrip at Kahuku Point for fighters and A-20 light bombers. While I was there my father died, but I didn't know about it since there was no telephone and Japanese Americans could not travel for the first three months after Pearl Harbor. I found out about my father the first time I went home. It's a good thing my father was not living — he would have gone to a concentration camp. They took all the fishermen and confiscated their boats, and the valley between Wahaiwa and Aiea became a concentration camp.

"February 1943, Japanese Americans were allowed to volunteer for Army service — 1,500 of us went to the Fort Shafter gymnasium, stripped naked and went through the physical exam. It was not much of a physical — I don't think they were even doctors. One neighbor, who was blind in one eye, was sent with us to Camp Shelby. When they found out at Shelby, they sent him home — but that's how lax the physical was!" Tsuda smiled.

The Nisei met fierce fighting at Lanuvio, where Tsuda's platoon was ordered to break out of a wooded area and advance across a wheat field toward a little railroad station.

"Lt. Fitzhugh was the first man to cross the road into field, but he was hit by German machine-gun fire coming down the road. The rest of us crossed without getting hit, but we were stuck in that wheat field almost eight hours — all the time harassed by 50 mm mortars: Boom, Boom, Boom! Tracer bullets from the road passed over us, so we couldn't raise our heads, and U.S. artillery started a fire in the wheat behind us, so we couldn't move forward or move back until sundown. The next morning we started the attack again — and the Germans were gone."

Tsuda was wounded by a mortar shell at Bruyères and spent 10 days at an evacuation hospital. Shrapnel he carries in his back today sets off alarms at airports and surprises doctors examining his X-rays, he says.

"When I returned to duty, the first sergeant of L Company was happy to see me, as he had only 20 men left on the line. We were sent to southern France, to the ridgeline along the border with Italy. The whole place was mined, and there were half a dozen dead Germans decomposing in the minefield. The only way to bring up supplies was by mule. One crazy mule broke off, ran into a mined area and blew up.

"From Marseilles, we were shipped to Leghorn, Italy. We attacked all the way up to Castello Poggio. One night we had two guards out, but the one on my side fell asleep. A German combat patrol came around very early in the morning and shot him in the face. I was here, and he was there," Tsuda said quietly, pointing an arm's length away, perhaps contemplating how fate had favored him that morning in 1945.

"The battle started in the dark and lasted until the sun came out, and we saw we had killed over 30 Germans in front of us. That same morning, they sent me on a five-day pass to Rome. I was there in Rome when the war ended."

On Tsuda's wall, a large wooden frame displays his sergeant's stripes, wartime photos and mementos. There, amid his many medals, is a Bronze Star, a Purple Heart, and the one he won't talk about; the one he earned that terrible morning at Castello Poggio: a Silver Star, its ribbon red, white and blue.

Hiro Asai

"One of our guys was killed on the last day of the war."

The town was tiny and the land bare when the Asai family first planted grapes here in the 1920's. Then came Prohibition, and they tore out the grapes and planted truck crops. "Booted out" in 1942 during the internment of Japanese Americans, they returned to the farm after the war. Peaches were hot, until the price dropped. Now the land is profitable and green with almond trees, 78 to an acre.

That is the history of a Japanese American farm family in Turlock, in California's Central Valley, as told by veteran Hiro Asai. On a warm October morning, Hiro and his wife, Hisa, reminisced as their son, Gary, drove the harvester between the rows of trees, raising clouds of dust and picking almonds bound for the Blue Diamond Co-op across the road. The powder-fine dust covered the trees' leaves and settled on everything, changing the color of a city visitor's white car to a desert tan. War in Europe seemed very far away, and talk of almonds and irrigation preceded Hiro's account of fighting in Italy with the 442nd Regimental Combat Team.

Asai joined the regiment as a replacement after the intense fighting in France, when the unit was ordered into the mountains of Italy, and combat became a succession of hill climbs under fire from fortified enemy positions. The Italian soldiers had stopped fighting when Italy agreed to an armistice in September 1943, but German troops occupied northern Italy and fought until the war ended in 1945.

"We never wore any insignia until after the war. We wore no stripes, no insignia — no unit designation or rank — nothing. Snipers look for that," he said.

"One of our guys was killed on the last day of the war," remembered Asai, himself wounded on the next-to-last day.

The Germans held one 8,000-foot Italian mountain that proved too steep for even mules to climb. It was up to the Nisei to carry up their mortar rounds and heavy supplies. One soldier was wounded as he walked to a spring to fill canteens, and it took six men to bring him down the mountain on a stretcher. The stretcher-bearers, unable to keep from sliding wildly down the steep slope, veered into bushes to slow their descent. Hiro said each time they hit a bush, the wounded man tumbled out of the stretcher screaming. Each time they would right themselves, put the wounded man back on the stretcher and slide further down the mountain until they were finally out of sight.

Soldiers had trouble finding drinking water in the mountains. At least once, each man had a single canteen of water to last four days. "Some men drank theirs fast; others would ration it. By the end, some guys were begging you for water."

Once, when the men had been without water for days, they found a pool with a dead horse in it. Although afraid of getting sick, they were desperate for water and, after some discussion, each man was allowed to take a single sip through a cloth strainer.

At war's end, Asai served in Pisa and Livorno, guarding POWs awaiting repatriation.

"We had nothing against them," Hiro said of the German prisoners. "The war was government fighting against government, but we treated each other as humans."

His family returned to Turlock from their war-long internment, and Hiro returned from Europe to find his older brother had taken over the family farm. That was the Japanese tradition. Hiro and another brother, Yoshio, teamed up to buy their own small farm. While Hiro went to trade school on the GI Bill and worked during the day repairing appliances, Hisa helped him run the farm, tend the irrigation and supervise the extra help they hired at harvest time. Their hard work had paid off. Now the farm's success depends on Gary and his wife, Becky.

The morning was gone; the talking had lasted to noon. Gary did not quit work to join in the tasty lunch Hisa prepared. Instead, he kept driving the harvester through lunchtime and, most likely, long after Hiro picked the last Asian pears of the season for his visitor and sent him back to the city in a dusty car.

Kenneth Hagino

"I had volunteered for combat, but suddenly I was in the wrong Army."

"My family had nine children, seven boys and two girls. I was the second. I'm 88, you see."

Kenneth Hagino began his story, and that of a unique Nisei Army unit of World War II, one that has never received the attention it deserves, the 1399th Construction Battalion.

"They called themselves 'Chowhounds' because they were always the first ones in line for chow!" he laughed.

No one would guess Hagino looked 88 years old, but when he later strolled around a local arboretum, he did so with some difficulty, backing up his claim.

Hagino's big family lived in Hilo, on the windward side of the Big Island of Hawaii, where his father worked as a longshoreman.

"You've heard about the strike, the one on the Hilo waterfront in the 1930s?" he asked. "My father got shot. He was in the hospital for a long time, but the union was good to us. They took care of the family and sent us food.

"I graduated Hilo High School in 1939, so I was age 20 when I enlisted. My father got very angry at me because I had the most schooling in our family and he expected me to stay home and work. After volunteering, we weren't allowed to go home, and we didn't know when the ship was coming, so we stayed in the armory in Hilo for a week or so. One ship had hit a mine on the Maui side, so that stopped all boat traffic for a while," Hagino said.

"There were 40 or 50 soldiers on our ship to Honolulu. We were all below deck, and on the upper decks were the priests and teachers they had arrested after Pearl Harbor, all on their way to prisons on the mainland. Some of the men had their own fathers up there, but didn't know it at the time.

"Although I had enlisted, they lumped me in with the 5th draft personnel. After two weeks of close-order drill at Schofield Barracks, they took all the Japanese American boys and had us picking up cigarette butts and trash along the highway. I had volunteered for combat, but suddenly I was in the wrong Army, the wrong place at the wrong time.

"We became the 1399th, all-Nisei, a mix of draftees and volunteers. The officers were of different races, but for Nisei, the highest rank allowed us was only warrant officer. We built Oahu defensive positions in Haleiwa, Aiea, all over the island. Not just coastal defenses, but roads and other projects, too.

In Wahiawa, we built one big water tank that is still there," Hagino said.

"They would assign different companies to different engineer groups. I was in Company B, assigned to 34th Engineer Regiment. The V.V.V., Varsity Victory Volunteers, was there at Schofield a few barracks away from us. They were all civilians. Later, when they were allowed, many volunteered for the 442 and MIS. Many volunteered from our outfit, too.

"I was surprised to see my brother, Masao, one day at Schofield. What are you doing here? 'Interpreter,' he said. He was a bright kid. They sent him to school for one year on the Mainland and then sent him to the Philippines, but the war ended and he went right to Tokyo. One of my younger brothers, Hiroshi, was a staff sergeant in the Korean War. He was a squad leader and was killed by accident by a soldier who had not unloaded his rifle," he sighed.

A basketball player in high school, Hagino joined the Chowhound team, which boasted several good athletes.

"One guy, Hasegawa, used to play pro baseball, and a couple others were state 100-yard dash champions. We won the Oahu championship of the Army Engineer League, and that was something because we were all Japanese Americans, and Japanese Americans were short guys! Men on other teams had played semi-pro on the mainland, and we beat them!" he boasted.

"After four years, officers asked, did I want to join the interpreters? Hell no! I said. I'm getting out! I worked for the state military department and joined the Hawaii National Guard. I later changed to the Reserve National Guard, which was forming different units, and worked there at the armory in Honolulu. I was sergeant first class. I finished at the University of Hawaii, studying finance on the GI Bill. After the University, I went to work at Manoa Finance Co.

"The 1399th dissolved at the end of the war. We don't meet much as a unit, but by accident, you come across soldiers you served with, and maybe three or four or five of us will get together.

"People won't remember the things we did — they take it for granted. It's just like that," he said.

Harold Kishaba

"Girls would bring out lemonade and pies for the POWs, but not the American soldiers."

Revealing his remarkable memory, machinist and welder Harold Kishaba recalls the numbers of all the locomotives he repaired. He also recalls his time as one of the original members of E Company of the 442nd Regimental Combat Team, from the training at Camp Shelby, Mississippi, to the fighting on Hill 140 in Italy and in the forests of France.

Maui is home to Kishaba, who reached the rank of sergeant, and except for the war years, he has lived there his entire life. His father landed in Maui after emigrating from Okinawa in 1919, his mother 12 years later. Kishaba attended St. Anthony Catholic School to the 10th grade, then trade school for another two years. His father raised hogs and his mother grew vegetables.

Kishaba could cut hair, and Camp Shelby's weekly inspections provided him with many willing customers. On Saturdays, the line for haircuts might be two hours long, and he had plenty of money left over, even after buying Coca-Cola for the barracks. He also bought fried chicken in Hattiesburg and brought it back on the bus in a mayonnaise jar or gallon jug.

"We sat in the back and pretended we didn't know where the smell was coming from. I would get back and wake up the boys. The barracks smelled like fried chicken." He grinned.

After basic training and maneuvers, 442nd soldiers were trucked to Dothan, Alabama, to guard Afrika Corps POWs, housed there in tents. So many farmers had joined the Army, POWs were needed to help with the peanut and cotton harvests. Kishaba's truck convoy stopped in the Alabama town of Andalusia so the soldiers could stretch their legs. Townspeople spotted the Nisei troops and thought Japan had attacked the United States and occupied the South. They ran inside and locked their doors.

Two soldiers guarding 12 prisoners traveled to the fields in each Army "six-by" truck. The POWs enjoyed three hot meals a day, while the Nisei survived on three meals of peanut butter and jelly, bologna and cheese, and ham sandwiches.

"Girls would bring out lemonade and pies for the POWs, but not the American soldiers," Kishaba said. "They liked the tall blonds and blue eyes. We asked, 'Don't you know that these guys were killing your uncles?!' They didn't know where Hawaii was. We'd ask, 'Did you hear of Pearl Harbor?' They thought Pearl Harbor was in the Philippines."

By the time the 442nd reached Hill 140 in Italy, slights from the Alabama locals were replaced with German artillery and machine-gun fire.

"We were ambushed," Kishaba said. "Many were wounded, and some lost their lives.

"Near the top of a hill one night, Germans came face to face with our 2nd squad — they walked right up to them and started talking German. All hell broke loose! We could see the tracers from a German machine gun. Our men would run underneath the tracers, fall down, get up and run again, and made their way back to the company."

Kishaba was later seriously wounded in the battle for Bruyères in the Vosges Mountains of France. Tree bursts from German artillery hit one of his buddies in a trench, burying him in pine branches. Kishaba chopped out the branches, pulled him out and bandaged him as best he could, only to be hit himself a short while later. When the battalion pulled back to Nice to recover from its heavy losses in the Vosges, he spent time in a hospital outside Paris and at a convalescent hospital in Plombières-les-Bains.

"Lost Battalion guys were stationed nearby. They saw me with the 442nd patch and treated me like a hero."

At the end of the war, Kishaba's unit processed German prisoners in Pisa, Italy, at a five-mile-square camp at the airport.

"Germans would uncrate boxes of weapons and supplies, clean off the cosmoline with gasoline and put it back in crates. I thought they would send it to the Pacific, but they sent it all out in the ocean and dumped it — millions of dollars' worth!

"Kelly Kuwayama was discharged early. His father had a Japanese grocery store, and he would send us boxes of *miso*, *shoyu*, dried cuttlefish and dried scallops." The men made their own pickled eggplant and salt cabbage, caught octopus and bought fish from the local Italian fishermen.

With a Purple Heart and a Bronze Star, Kishaba does not consider himself a hero, but remembers those who are. He said some believe the 442nd men were awarded lesser medals than soldiers in other units. Hawaii, not yet a state, had no congressmen, and no one to push Medal of Honor nominations. Veterans went unrecognized and widows uncompensated, he said.

Henry Hayashi

"I don't know how I survived."

It's his smile you notice first: broad and true, and nearly omnipresent. And after talking just a few minutes with Henry Hayashi, you get the feeling he is a "glass half-full" sort of man. Even his accounts of combat and racism, however grim, end with a sense of optimism — and a smile. Hayashi sat with a few friends at the annual reunion for 100th Infantry Battalion veterans, this one in Las Vegas. Every year fewer veterans attend.

"I never did go to camp. I enlisted in 1941, before the war, thinking I would serve for one year," the 94-year-old began. "At that time, there was no racism in the Army. Six of us were sent to auto mechanics school at the Presidio of San Francisco. After Pearl Harbor, they didn't really trust us, and there was more discrimination than before. The Nisei were sent out of the Presidio."

In the maintenance battalion, his technician rating as a mechanic had earned him $72 a month, but when Hayashi was sent to Fort Sheridan, outside Chicago, and busted in rank to private first class, his monthly pay fell to $36. Hayashi's parents and younger brothers were ordered from their home in Los Angeles to the Amache internment camp in Colorado.

Hayashi and other Nisei were sent to Camp Shelby, Mississippi, about the time the 100th Battalion arrived there from Camp McCoy and prepared to go overseas.

"We couldn't join the 100th at that time," Hayashi explained. "They already had too much training for us to catch up."

Instead, Hayashi remained at Camp Shelby, training the new 442nd soldiers, and rose in rank to sergeant. He shipped overseas at the end of 1944.

"I joined the 100th Battalion at the best possible time — I missed all the heavy fighting at the Lost Battalion. Those guys were all 18-year-old kids, just out of high school."

This comment got the attention of his friend from Seattle, Frank Nishimura.

"I was young when I went in. I got real old," Nishimura said. "I was the youngest guy in the outfit — they called me 'Junior.' By the end of the war I was the oldest, due to all the casualties."

Hayashi continued. "I was lucky: all my officers were Japanese Americans who had worked their way up. You could not find better officers. Alan Ohata got the Medal of Honor. Fred Kanemura, my platoon leader, a Silver Star."

He remembers one day when he found luck on his side.

"This was the battle where Sadao Munemori got the Medal of Honor. [Munemori was the first Nisei to earn the Medal of Honor in World War II, by jumping on an enemy grenade to save his fellow soldiers. The medal was awarded posthumously.] Munemori was in A Company, and I was a platoon sergeant in B Company. We were attacking a hill and were pinned down. Finally A Company was able to take their position and we moved around them. That's when we hit the minefield. We lost three, and three more got wounded when a string of about nine mines went off. I don't know how I survived that minefield, but we got out.

"I don't know how I survived," he quietly repeated to himself.

K. Kobashi, another 100th veteran, recalled his own luck that day.

"I was next to Sadao Munemori when he died. I called for the medic. Actually, he saved my life."

Hayashi said, "At the end of the war many of us went to school in Florence. I studied agriculture. The black market was everywhere — soldiers were selling clothes, boots, everything you can imagine. I think someone even sold an Army truck!

"We got back home, and I couldn't believe the discrimination, worse than before the war! No one would hire us. I took up landscaping, the only job I could get. We bought our home in 1948, and five lots butted up against us — all Caucasians. No sooner did we move in, you should have seen the For Sale signs go up! But it was a good thing," he said, finding another glass half-full. "It allowed young Japanese American families to move in — two of them were veterans."

Henry's children, Sharon, Gayle, and Robert, grandchildren and 12 great-grandchildren live nearby. The three kids and his wife, Elsie, accompanied Henry to the reunion.

"Lots of happy memories, lots of sad memories," he said, managing a smile.

"We don't talk much about the bad things, about combat," he observed. "But still, the sad things seem like they happened yesterday."

Henry Nakada

"My mother was quite famous for having seven sons in the Army during World War II."

Twenty miles east of Los Angeles, Azusa was once green with lemon and orange groves and truck farms.

"It used to be a beautiful valley," Henry Nakada said, remembering his childhood home.

Henry was the fifth of 12 kids. Everyone worked on the farm. The little kids would irrigate, or follow behind a horse cultivating a field, or go out and pick crops. A three-room schoolhouse handled grades one through eight.

He was 18 when the war broke out. Older brothers, Saburo and Yoshinao, had already graduated college and been drafted before Pearl Harbor.

"My mother was quite famous for having seven sons in the Army during World War II. It hit the Associated Press and she got letters from mothers from all over the United States. Yoshinao was in one of the early cadres of the 442nd. Saburo, Minoru, Jimmy, John and Steven all joined the MIS."

Before the war, it had been hard to find work in California, where many jobs paid only 25 cents an hour. Nakada needed money for college, and he learned he could make $1.25 an hour in Alaska. He ended up in Anchorage, working construction at Fort Richardson and at Elmendorf Air Force Base.

"It took me a whole day to get a job," he deadpanned.

"When the war broke out, they fired me immediately, because I was Japanese American. I was disappointed, but not surprised," he said. He soon learned that back in California, his parents were being held in stables at the Pomona Fairgrounds.

"I'll tell you a story." He smiled and leaned forward in a conspiratorial posture. "Technically, Japanese Americans were not allowed to be drafted. The G-2 Intelligence officer in charge of the Japanese Americans in Alaska knew me and said, 'Goddammit, Nakada, you're about as American as anyone I ever met. If you were 21, I'd get you drafted tomorrow.'

"'Sir, I just turned 21,' I told him."

As the officer promised, the next day Nakada was sent to Fort Richardson. After basic training, he transferred to Fort Sheridan, Illinois, to mechanics school.

"It was March or April 1943, they shipped me to Camp Shelby to the 442nd. When we went after the Lost Battalion, 3rd Battalion was the lead battalion, with I Company first. Me and two others were on point, one was killed, one was wounded, I jumped under a holly bush. We were 75–100 yards ahead of the company in an area covered by moss and tundra. The Germans were dug in. There was a machine gun 25 feet above me, and there were three machine guns in front of us."

Nakada survived the close call but the rescue mission continued unabated.

"It was two to three days later when Barney Hajiro made his famous charge. The day after the big charge, we lost many men, but so did the Germans, so they withdrew. I was one of the point men in the patrol to meet the Lost Battalion, with Mutt Sakumoto and Fred Ugai. Mutt saw them first. I know they were happier than hell. We weren't there 15 minutes, talking to the Lost Battalion, we were ordered to take the next hill, then the next hill. Not that we could have done anything — we were a third of a company. If the Germans knew, they could have punched through us. We took about six or seven more hills. Second Platoon was gone. First and 2nd together had 10 guys, 3rd the same. There couldn't have been more than a platoon left, and some general says, 'Take the next hill.'

"Larry Chinen and I were the only men left in 1st and 2nd Platoons. I left with trench foot, and he's still mad at me for leaving — even today, 60 years later. He doesn't want to talk to me. He doesn't talk to anyone."

Nakada spent five weeks in a French hospital before rejoining his unit.

After the war, Nakada attended Temple University, in Philadelphia, and married Mitsu, a girl he knew from church back home.

"After ten years in Philadelphia, they kicked me out with a PhD," he laughed. He spent a career in biochemistry in California.

"Then I decided it's time I got back to Alaska. I retired at 55 and became a commercial fisherman, netting salmon on Prince William Sound."

Nakada has two sons in Alaska and one in Hawaii. His granddaughter, Tela, was the first woman on the U.S. Olympic Wrestling Team, and competed in the Athens Olympics.

"She wrestled mostly boys, and on top of that, she's beautiful. That's her Grandpa's opinion!"

George T. Sakato

"I did something I shouldn't have done."

Troop ships carrying replacements for the 442nd sailed out of Newport News, Virginia. They ran north, then south — zigzagging. It made for a long voyage, but it was their best chance of avoiding the enemy's frightening submarine wolfpacks and torpedoes. Fast escort vessels ran between the troopships, dropping depth charges, but German U-boats still sank three ships during the month-long crossing to Oran, Algeria.

"To kill time, we'd tap 50-cent pieces with a tablespoon until they flattened out and got smaller. Then we cut out the centers and made rings," George T. Sakato remembers.

After ships were torpedoed, the Nisei soldiers quit making rings, afraid their tapping sounds had attracted the submarines.

Animated and comedic, George Sakato surveys each new face for the person's intentions before smiling and joking and laughing in a little cackle that somehow fits his compact form. As a medal recipient, he is repeatedly tracked down by journalists, well-wishers and the curious. His life has become a near-continuous journey from his Denver home to an apparently endless series of events and speeches. His daughter Leslie accompanies him. He never says no.

Sakato says he has always been called "Joe," due in part to his father's poor English. His father saw "Geo." and liked it, not realizing it was an abbreviation of "George."

When America entered the war, Sakato wanted to join the Army Air Corps, but, like other Nisei, he was turned down. He was eventually allowed to join the 442nd, instead, when restrictions against Japanese Americans were lifted in 1943.

Sakato met up with Easy Company in Pisa and they soon shipped out to France, attached to the 7th Army's 36th Division. The men went into action attacking the town of Bruyères. Sakato surprised an enemy soldier and officer, took them prisoner and kept the officer's Luger pistol, a prized souvenir among the GIs.

A few days later, the unit tried to advance across a field adjacent to a railroad track — a principal supply line the Germans heavily guarded. Enemy mortar positions and machine guns controlled the open fields from a rocky prominence, Hill 617. Sakato's platoon was trucked behind the Germans and then walked all night to get into position to attack the hill.

They attacked at dawn and took the Germans by surprise. They sent the German prisoners to the rear, only to find out

that there was no "rear" — the Americans had been surrounded. The situation quickly turned desperate. Artillery fire started coming in, and men jumped into the same foxholes the enemy had just vacated. Sakato had used up all his ammunition. Enemy soldiers were moving up the hill behind them. Medic Kelly Kuwayama was hit as he tended a wounded man.

"I did something I shouldn't have done. I was mad. I was out of my mind," he said, emotional after so many years.

He grabbed a German Mauser and shot it until it was empty, then used his grenades, then the captured Luger. When he saw his buddy Saburo Tanamachi killed, he furiously charged up the hill. Men followed him and they retook the hill.

A few days later, Sakato was surprised by a quick visit from his older brother, Henry, a soldier in the 100th Battalion stationed on a neighboring hillside. The day after their visit, a piece of shrapnel bounced off Sakato's spine and lodged in his lung. He spent months going from hospital to hospital, first in England, and then across the United States. Army doctors determined the shrapnel was too dangerous to remove — it is still there.

He never returned to his unit, and, without other news, the men figured he had died. (When Sakato appeared at their first reunion in 1958, one man exclaimed, "Am I looking at a ghost?") He was about to be discharged from a hospital in San Diego when an officer pinned the Distinguished Service Cross on him. Squad leader Tsune Takemoto had written him up for a citation.

When he visited Bruyères in 1994, townspeople took him to see Hill 617. It looked different — the little trees he remembered had grown up around the hill.

"They can never be cut down. It would ruin the saws," the Frenchmen told him. "They are full of shrapnel."

Years later, retired from a career with the post office, the telephone rang at his home in Denver.

"We want you to come to Washington," the voice said. "We are going to upgrade your medal."

Always ready with a joke, for once Sakato was speechless.

He traveled with Leslie and his wife Bess to Washington, D.C., and on June 21, 2000, in a Rose Garden ceremony, and after 55 years, President Bill Clinton awarded the Medal of Honor to George T. "Joe" Sakato.

Leighton "Goro" Sumida

"People won't remember the things we did."

Nearly every day, veterans meet at the 100th Battalion Club-house, on a small street across from Honolulu's Iolani School. They spend time with their buddies, "talk story" and maybe enjoy a potluck lunch together. One frequent visitor is Leighton Sumida, an original 100th Battalion veteran who served with the unit throughout the war. The wiry 90-year-old says he is one of the club's youngest members. He underwent triple-bypass surgery last year, and was back at the club in a week. Goro, as he is known, is a joker, and possesses a keen memory, making for colorful stories and a unique look at history.

"Our family had seven boys, and six went in the service," Sumida said. "Three were interpreters — one went to Burma, one Virginia, and the youngest one was in the Korean War; one was in the 1399th 'Chowhounds,' and my kid brother served in Guam. In the 100th, we had two Sumidas, and later on, I saw the other guy got killed.

"Pearl Harbor? I was working as a carpenter, and I didn't have to go to war, but 14 days after the war broke out, I was in. It was supposed to be 14 months, but I got stuck for four years!" Sumida laughed.

"We went through basic training at Schofield Barracks, living in tents. They gave us rifles and one clip, six rounds. They thought Japanese Americans might sabotage or something, but how were we supposed to stop the enemy with six rounds? June 1942, we left from Pier 16 on a ship to Oakland. I was sick like a demon and stayed on deck sucking an orange. I couldn't go down to do KP, so I paid another guy to do it for me.

"We took the train to Camp McCoy, the train curtains down the whole way, and I was still sick. The conductor saw I was white and not eating, so he let me lie down — same with another sick guy. We saw our first snowfall at McCoy and built our first snowman."

The men were moved to Camp Shelby, Mississippi, and conducted maneuvers in Louisiana and Texas, returning to Shelby as the new 442nd men were just arriving.

"Next thing you know, we are on a troopship from New Jersey to Oran, Algeria. Oran was filthy. I got hives from drinking the brackish water. Hot in the day, cold at night — that was Oran. We stayed about a week and moved from there to Italy — Salerno — the first place the 34th Division landed," he remembered.

"Salerno was where we started, where we went into combat. There were about 1,000 men in the first wave. The Germans let the first and second waves come in, and then opened up with machine guns and artillery. They had been there for a while and they had a lot of places zeroed in. Italy was all hills, and the Germans were on the top of the hills. We always started at the bottom.

A few of Sumida's memories made him laugh.

"We Hawaiians, we are crazy! We went swimming in our BVDs, just like in Hawaii. We used to hide in the bushes, gamble, drink beer — all happy-go-lucky. We had 40 men in our platoon, all with only one stripe. That's good! It means you can only get busted one stripe!"

The platoon had begun to sound like a bunch of high school pranksters until Sumida held out a photo of the men and the stories turned grim.

"All these guys are dead," he said.

Sumida said he might have been killed himself on seven occasions, once when his own B.A.R. man missed him by three inches. Another time, mortar rounds came in as he helped a scared, 17-year-old kid dig a foxhole. The first explosion buried the kid so completely, only his two legs stuck out of the dirt. Sumida pulled him out.

"A guy from Kauai got shot in the stomach and was left out by himself all night," he said. "When we found him, he was holding his own guts in. He was the first E Company man to die. Just before Cassino, at Hill 940, we carried a 185-pound guy five miles. We had to carry him through a minefield, but he was still dragging on the ground!

"Saburo Hasagawa was hit at Cassino and lost a leg. He just died a month ago. He was 98. His kid brother was killed when he stuck his head up to see where an artillery shell landed.

"So, it's like that," Sumida said. "People won't remember the things we did. They take it for granted."

Melvin Mutsuo Muramoto

"We walked all the way up to Lyons."

Melvin Muramoto is a St. Louis fan — the Cardinals, the Rams — you can count on that as much as you can his silver hair and his omnipresent smile. Only the neat haircut hints of some time in the military, of the young man who fought across Italy and France with the U.S. Army's famed 442nd Regimental Combat Team.

One of eight seniors in his Hilo High School class, Muramoto volunteered for the Army. (Hideo Luna, the class president, also volunteered. He was killed his first week in combat.) The initial Nisei volunteers reported to Schofield Barracks on Oahu on March 27th, 1943. They were issued full equipment and ordered to take the 100-pound duffels to the boat.

"We had to carry them all the way to Mississippi, to Camp Shelby," he said, still in disbelief a half century later.

The Queen Mary carried the recruits to San Francisco. There they left the luxury liner and moved to a train for the long trip to Camp Shelby. The "cattle cars" they occupied had no bathrooms. Men jumped off the slow-moving train and into the bushes to relieve themselves.

The 442nd was assigned its own area in sprawling Camp Shelby. The men found the typical GI food to be strange, and the cook in Muramoto's barracks, Goichi Nagao, traded with others for more of the rice the men craved.

"And he had the key to the kitchen if we got hungry at night," Muramoto said, laughing.

"The other guys looked out for me since I was the youngest — just 18. Most were in their 20s. Being the youngest though, sometimes you get a lot of abuse."

The men sailed to Italy and went into action north of Rome, where they assaulted Hill 140, a German stronghold and the scene of their first sustained combat. The first night, Sgt. Masamori Kushi was wounded as Muramoto's squad patrolled a hillside.

"He was a big guy, very intelligent, and one of the top golfers in Hilo. I felt terrible when I saw him wounded in the hand, chest, out the back. We had to carry him from one hill to another.

"It seems like we were always on night patrol. Being the youngest, I guess, I was always the scout. Once, the squad leader, assistant squad leader and I went down to a water hole to fill canteens, and the Germans had the water hole zeroed-in."

A blast split Muramoto's helmet and knocked him out. He spent three days in the hospital before returning to combat.

The men replaced British troops in Florence, then returned to the coast for two weeks in Pisa before pulling back to stage for the invasion of southern France. Rain soaked them as they rode the landing craft to shore.

"We walked all the way up to Lyons. It was terrible walking in the pouring rain."

Muramoto was wounded again in the fierce fighting for the village of Bruyères. No place was safe, as German 88s fired into the trees, sending shrapnel onto the soldiers below. He was hit in the back and spent two weeks in the hospital at Plombières-les-Bains. He learned the same barrage had killed his best friend.

Following the weeks of fighting in the Vosges, the 442nd manned the Maginot Line in southern France to defend against an invasion by the German troops who still occupied northern Italy.

After his discharge at Schofield Barracks, Muramoto took his first plane ride on the way home to Hilo — the plane full of returning Nisei veterans. He spent a year in Hilo working at his brother's service station and soon met Janet, his wife-to-be. He attended the University of Missouri — where he became a St. Louis fan — then went to work making maps for the U.S. Army for 26 years.

The family moved to northern California, where Muramoto, ready for a new career, opened an orthodontics lab. He retired in Sacramento, enjoys watching his football, his yard full of fruit trees, and children and grandchildren, who live nearby.

Bill Thompson

"No one expected the war to start here."

"There is no place more beautiful than Hilo after a rain," said veteran Bill Thompson, smiling. He grew up there, on the windward, rainy side of the "Big Island" of Hawaii.

"The Big Island was all sugarcane, and small coffee farms on the Kona side. My father was a blacksmith and welder, fixing machinery on the plantations and for Hawaii Consolidated Railroad, on the Hamakua coast. He emigrated from Scotland via Canada and married my mother, a Nisei who was born in Hawaii.

"Hilo was like country living. Life was really easy and enjoyable for us kids. We all went to Japanese School — but I've forgotten my Japanese already. We graduated high school in June '41. December '41 was Pearl Harbor. The newspapers said what the Japanese were doing in the Orient, but we never expected it in Hawaii. No one expected the war to start here."

According to Thompson, the laconic island atmosphere turned tense after Pearl Harbor: Hilo was shelled by a submarine, as was Nawiliwili, a port on Kauai. The shelling of Hilo woke the town and left a hole in the pier.

"The Japanese were trying to show they were still around," Thompson said.

As he began to speak about the war, his beaming smile appeared only once or twice.

"Lt. Gen. Delos Emmons took over as military governor after the failure of Gen. Short at Pearl Harbor. Emmons had a direct order to send the Japanese American population to the island of Molokai and confine them there, but he sat on the order until FDR changed his mind. Actually, his original order was to send us to the Mainland, and Emmons replied, 'My ships are tied up.' That was the difference between him and Gen. DeWitt in San Francisco. Even Gen. MacArthur said he wanted to use the Nisei, not like DeWitt, that crazy general in California who wanted to lock them up.

"The Nisei were reclassified 'enemy alien,' so we could forget about being drafted. The 100th Battalion had already been formed, and the Army moved the 100th out of Hawaii, as they were not sure of their loyalty if the Japanese invaded. June 5 or 6, 1942, they shipped them to Wisconsin, and the paper said the Wisconsin people were taking the 100th boys home for dinner and nice things like that.

"My brother George was drafted before World War II and was stationed on Oahu at Schofield Barracks. He volunteered for the 442nd and served with the regiment's 522nd Field Artillery Battalion. When the call came, my brother James and I volunteered for the 442nd. After training at Camp Shelby, James went to the 100th Battalion as a replacement, and I went to Headquarters Company of the 442nd's 2nd Battalion."

Thompson served with the Headquarters Company Anti-tank Platoon. The regiment had a full anti-tank company, and each of the 442nd's infantry battalions had an anti-tank platoon with three 57 mm guns, "what the British called a 'six-pounder,'" he explained. "Once you fired, your position was exposed, and you had to decide whether to shoot again or to get out of the way."

The war over, Thompson left Europe in the early part of November 1945, spending 20 days crossing the Atlantic, just the start of his long trip back to Hilo.

"I spent a day or so in Schofield, where we got what they called a 'ruptured duck' pin, showing we had been honorably discharged. It was supposed to be an eagle pin, but it looked like a ruptured duck.

"My mind was made up to take advantage of the GI Bill of Rights and go to University of Hawaii. Many 442nd guys took advantage of the GI Bill. The 100th boys had a harder time — it had been five years or so, and it was harder for them to go back to school, but they had priority for civil service jobs. I wanted to be an architect but ended up being a civil engineer. Good thing I didn't become an architect: I discovered I was colorblind. I could never sit down with the client and talk about a paint scheme," he said, smiling.

Thompson served as president of the 442nd Veterans Club in Honolulu. "The 442 Club started in 1946, right after the war," he said.

"I believe if you are an American, you're an American. Period! You are entitled to all rights as citizens.

"'Americanism is about mind and heart and not about race,' that is what FDR said, and I tell people, that is what we proved as soldiers. We feel good that what we did is part of American history."

Denis Teraoka

"That's how it happens. C'est la guerre."

Recalling the old Hawaii of his younger days, Denis Teraoka had to smile. So much had changed since the retired Honolulu dentist grew up on the Paauhau Plantation, at Honokaa town on the Big Island. His family of 10 children — seven boys and three girls — produced six U.S. Army veterans. During World War II, Denis and his late brother Mutsuo both served in Europe; Hisao served in the segregated 1399th Engineers in Hawaii, and James in the Pacific Theater. Brothers Hiroshi and Munoe served in the Korean War; only his brother Bob stayed home, shouldering the responsibility of caring for their parents. Denis talked about his experiences in the 100th Infantry Battalion, and of a Hawaii quite different from the beaches of Waikiki.

"The plantation manager, he was the big shot. We had to listen to him, because we worried about getting kicked out. He had the attitude, 'Even if you have an education, you will come back and work on the plantation.' This was in the 1930s. I came to Honolulu for my schooling and I went to University of Hawaii, where I had two years of Basic ROTC, then two years of Advanced. When I graduated, I went back to the plantation with the idea I would work in the chemistry department lab, since I went to UH. But they ignored that, so I cut sugarcane for a year."

Teraoka had earned a commission in the Army Reserve upon completing the ROTC program. He enrolled in Western Dental College in Kansas City, Missouri. He was surprised by a draft notice in April 1942 — no one knew he was in Kansas City, he thought. His induction was deferred until he graduated in September 1943, and he reported to Camp Shelby. There was no thought of visiting his family in Hawaii, as there was no longer civilian transportation to the Islands. A second lieutenant, he began training with D Company, a heavy weapons unit. In April 1944, Teraoka joined two other officers and 100 enlisted men, all replacements for the 100th Battalion. They sailed for Naples and met the battalion at Anzio.

"The 100th got wiped out in Cassino and had just come to Anzio to regroup. We stayed there about a month, before our next battles. On June 5, 1944, we saw the high rises of Rome and thought we were going to capture the city, but they stopped us and let other troops through. The next morning, we went to Civitavecchia and met the 442nd, which had just arrived. We saw all our friends, and I ran into my brother, Mutsuo, in H Company.

"We tried to tell the 442nd boys what it was like to be in combat, but they didn't want to hear it. We went into battle in Sasseta. The 100th gave a good account of ourselves — we earned a Presidential Unit Citation — the new 442nd didn't do too well.

"We boarded a ship at Leghorn, and the word was we are going home. Instead, we sailed to Marseille and they told us we were going to the Vosges. In those Vosges Mountains, it was cold, wet, raining all the time. You never saw the sun. Biffontaine, Belmont and Bruyères — we liberated those three towns, rested only two days and they told us to pack up — we are going out to rescue the Lost Battalion. The Lost Battalion was cut off, short of food, ammunition and clothing. We kept going, and after four days and four nights we broke through, but some companies had been decimated. Like many of us, I developed trench foot. I went to the aid station and there was a long line of enlisted men, so I let them all go first."

Teraoka continued. "In April 1945, we got aboard ship again and we all thought now we are ready to go home. Instead, we sailed to Italy and back into combat. We got to one little town and sent out scouts while we rested. A truck from C Company waited with us. They had one soldier, only about as tall as his rifle. He had a grenade hanging on his shoulder strap. He sat there, a few feet from me. Ten seconds later, BOOM, the grenade went off. Everyone yelled, 'Take cover! Enemy fire!'

"We looked at the soldier. He straightened up. 'Mother!' he cried, and he fell back — that was it. Dead. And you know, the next day was the end of the war in Italy.

"That's how it happens. C'est la guerre.

"In April 1946, word came down, the 442nd is going home! It took us six days to New York City. While we were there, girls came around for dancing. I met a girl named Joy, got engaged in one week's time and she became my wife!"

Ayato Kiyomoto

"We were there to prove ourselves."

Ayato Kiyomoto sat on a park bench on the broad shoulder of a volcano, looking out over the fertile green slopes down to the white resort hotels dotting Maui's Wailea Coast. He was born here, and this was home, a scene he had viewed 10,000 times, and from it, he drew the strength to relive old memories of family and a long-ago war.

Throughout his childhood, the family's farm was full with the vegetables, chickens and pigs they raised, but Ayato's mother told him their first six months on the farm they survived on only the grasses they could pick. His parents arrived from Japan in 1902, his father working in the fields until he could afford a farm of his own. After a year, his oldest brother was born. The family grew to include eight children.

The attack that shook Hawaii ignited Ayato's patriotism. He volunteered near the end of 1942, entered the Army on March 23, 1943, and was sent to the 442nd. He was 22 years old.

"We had something to do. We were there to prove ourselves," he said.

"It was the end of April, I believe, when we left Camp Shelby and boarded a train to Norfolk, Virginia, to go overseas. Rumor had about 100 ships in the convoy. The first few days, 20–30 percent of us were seasick to the point of being bedridden. It was 28 days to Naples, where the harbor had sunken ships and bomb damage. We lived in pup tents in a cattle pasture. We were there for three weeks before we were called to action."

Ayato was wounded twice in Italy, spending two months in the Third General Hospital in Rome. When he was fit to return to combat, the Nisei were sent to France, and after 16 days in combat, he was wounded again while directing a tank against a sniper position in a little town past Bruyères. A bullet hit his forearm, shattering the bone and sending him to a hospital in Aix-en-Provence for six months.

Prior to the fighting in Bruyères, he remembers his squad occupied a French home for three days, while the old woman who lived there stayed in the cellar. Near the house, the soldiers discovered a German pistol and a branch-covered trench that looked suspicious. They investigated and found a German. The skinny soldier wore a long beard and suffered from gangrene. He had been in there for several days without food or water.

"A couple days later we went into combat," Ayato said. "That's when I got wounded."

In the medical tent, he saw the German soldier, whose leg and arm had been amputated.

"He recognized me and held his hand like he was praying and thanked me for saving his life. He said I saved his life."

Ayato paused, silent for a time.

"You had a sense of Aloha."

He departed Europe on a British troopship, and remembered the food being much better than on the voyage over. Back on Maui and unable to do construction work because of his war wounds, he found work at a farmers' co-op, beginning a long career selling and wholesaling produce.

One day an Issei man surprised him by asking about his time in combat.

"Is shooting a German like shooting a pheasant?"

"I was shocked," Ayato said, unable to offer a reply.

"I could not insult an elder. I just walked away from him."

Frank Mizufuka

"We weren't over there fighting for just the heck of it."

Yuki the dog is generously spoiled. The google-eyed Chihuahua mix is nervous and yippy, only content in the arms of his owner, Frank Mizufuka.

Mizufuka is 89 but does not look it, perhaps because of his lifelong participation in athletics. Before World War II, he was a football player and championship wrestler at Fullerton College in California and tried out for the Olympic wrestling team. As a gentle man who later sold San Francisco memorabilia to tourists, few would guess the unassuming shopkeeper was missing a couple ribs, wounded on a French battlefield while volunteering to assault an enemy tank.

In 1942, Mizufuka was a young man when his family was ordered to the Rohwer Relocation Center in rural Arkansas. He was there only briefly before being drafted.

"As a civilian, even though we were discriminated against, we took it in stride. We had no power and no one to represent us. We thought that was normal," he said.

"After a year and a half in the service, I was working as a clerk in the personnel office in Fort Robinson, Arkansas. The 442nd was getting so beat up in Italy, they asked for volunteer replacements. That's when I volunteered for combat. I was a sergeant, but I gave up my stripes to go overseas. I was a clerk, not an infantryman, and I did not want to be a sergeant and lead men in combat!"

Within two weeks of Mizufuka arriving in Italy, the Nisei were sent to France and into combat in the Vosges Mountains. Six days later he was wounded.

During the October fighting in the Vosges, the 442nd F and L Companies formed the O'Connor Task Force, named for its leader, Maj. Emmett L. O'Connor. The two companies advanced through the forest at night in a flanking action designed to envelop enemy forces.

"I didn't know anybody, just the man ahead of me and the man behind, and I began to fear — so many guys were getting wounded and killed," he said. "The German 88 mm fired timed shells that burst at a certain distance and were more dangerous than those exploding on the ground. They hit the trees, you see, that was the thing that was devastating because of the shrapnel."

Mizufuka was the man in his squad who, in addition to his rifle, carried a bazooka, a rocket-firing weapon used against tanks and other vehicles. The bazooka's hollow metal tube was not heavy, but long and awkward to handle, Mizufuka said. The vest he wore carrying the rockets was heavy, and Tito Okamoto, his diminutive assistant, carried more rockets and loaded each one for him to fire. Mizufuka was assigned the weapon with no previous training.

"They usually just picked a big guy to carry it," he said.

"We were being shelled by an 88 on a tank. Tanks didn't usually waste their shells on infantry, but the Germans were protecting their homeland and had their backs to the wall. The tank was holding us up because we couldn't cross the valley without him seeing us. I volunteered to go after him. We crawled, he shot at us and the second shot burst and hit me right in the chest, and here," pointing to scars on his arm.

"The doctors wouldn't operate on me. They said I had to go back to the States but wouldn't let me fly because of my lung wound. So I sweated out seven months before I could get on a hospital ship. After the surgery, I spent four more months recovering."

Mizufuka has begun writing his autobiography because he wants nieces and nephews to know his story. He says they only know he was in the 442nd, but not that he was wounded, earned a Bronze Star, or any other details. There are things he thinks they should know.

"We weren't just over there fighting for just the heck of it, we were fighting for a cause!" he wants them to know. "For those of us who made the supreme sacrifice, we did not sacrifice ourselves in vain. What we did is why you are now better off in our society, with better jobs and positions of leadership. The ventures you undertake and fulfill are partly due to the record we set before you were born."

Mizufuka gazed across the room, the little dog asleep in his arms.

"Many of us at that time were not considered ordinary members of society, and the only way to overcome that was to show we are no different from any others. We wanted to do whatever it took to overcome the obstacles we had to endure. Not only for ourselves, but for our children and our children's children."

Tom S. Takata

"One German soldier, surrendering, tripped a wire and lost a leg."

Tom Takata was a quiet man, one who was well liked and respected by his comrades. Modest as well as quiet, he did not rush to tell his story, but after some encouragement, he talked about his time as a squad leader in the 442nd Regimental Combat Team.

He grew up in Sacramento, where his family ran a vegetable stand and grocery store. By 1941, he knew his draft number would be coming up soon, so he decided to enlist, hoping to serve in the Army coastal artillery. He enlisted on July 8th and was sent to Camp Walters, Texas, for basic training.

"It was very hot in Texas and hard on the kids from Seattle," Takata recalled.

Next came the Army's massive war games, the Louisiana Maneuvers, and then Takata went on to Fort Jackson, South Carolina, where the 121st Regiment was assigned to protect the coastline.

It was at Fort Jackson that he heard about Pearl Harbor and, later, learned his family had been sent to the Tule Lake Relocation Center in remote northern California. It was 1943 before he was allowed to visit them, making the long trip by train and bus via Reno, Nevada, and Klamath Falls, Oregon. Takata's older brother was at the camp with his four kids, and his sister was living there with his parents. His visit lasted about ten days.

He served at Fort Leonard Wood, Missouri, until his 8th Division moved on to California for desert maneuvers, leaving behind Takata and a dozen other Nisei soldiers who could not enter the West Coast exclusion zone. Soon other Nisei joined them in a personnel holding pattern termed "Detached Men, Enlisted." In spite of this official segregation, Takata said he never experienced hostility from other soldiers because of his Japanese ancestry.

Takata volunteered for the 442nd and, although he was a staff sergeant, had to repeat basic training, this time at Fort McClelland, Alabama. The Nisei in training numbered "about a battalion — mostly people already in the Army," he said. He was originally assigned to B Company, 100th Battalion, but the 100th had too many sergeants and sent him to E Company, 2nd Battalion. He joined the company in Italy just before the troops sailed for France and the fierce fighting in the rugged Vosges Mountains.

The veterans joke about the so-called "Champagne Campaign," the misleading nickname for the months spent patrolling the mountainous border between France and Italy. While the duty was supposed to be a break for the combat infantrymen while they rebuilt their ranks following the fighting in the Vosges, clashes with enemy patrols were common, and several men were killed or wounded. Soldiers set out mines and tripwires on the steep slopes of Mount Grosso, above Sospel, France, Takata remembered.

"One German soldier — surrendering — tripped a wire and lost a leg," he said. "We would go on 'Cabbage Patrols.' A patrol would go out and bring cabbage on the way home. I was hit by a mortar shell while repairing communication cable — Kelly patched me up," he said, referring to medic Kelly Yeiichi Kuwayama.

The Nisei guarded POWs in Italy long after the end of the war, until finally, in November 1945, Takata headed back to the States. The ship circled around a huge storm in the Atlantic, stretching the trip to Newport News to 21 days.

"Other guys who were on an aircraft carrier got home in five days," Takata said.

He was discharged at Camp Grant, Illinois, and when he got back to California, he found his family living in Petaluma with an uncle who ran a chicken farm. The family moved back to Sacramento where Takata worked for a year at the Army depot, then took a job with the state of California. He was working for the state when he met his wife Rose.

"Then my brother started a produce business and the whole family worked on that," he said. By the time he retired, he had worked in the produce business almost 28 years.

More than 60 years had passed since the fighting in France, but medic Kelly Kuwayama remembered Takata well, paying him perhaps the highest compliment one soldier can give another.

"You could always depend on Tom," he said.

Shigeru T. Kizuka

"The man that got killed when I got wounded? I didn't even know his name."

April 1945. Love Company, 2nd Platoon was pinned down by enemy mortar fire. Pvt. Shigeru Kizuka had joined the 3rd Battalion of the 442nd Regimental Combat Team the previous November, but he was still a novice. Much of his time with the unit had been on patrol duty along the French-Italian border, while the Nisei were rebuilding after the deadly battle rescuing the Lost Battalion.

As he cautiously stuck his head up to get his bearings, a bullet dented his helmet — not wounding him — but bringing him one step closer to being "a veteran." He collected his wits and reminded himself that young replacements were routinely killed or wounded before they gained the skills to survive in combat.

Kizuka's father, Tokushige Kizuka, was active in the Japanese American community in Watsonville, California. (Today, a community hall there bears his name.) The day after Pearl Harbor, he was arrested by the FBI and imprisoned; the family did not learn his fate for several weeks. With the rest of his family, Kizuka was sent to Arizona to the Poston II relocation camp on July 4th, 1942.

He first volunteered for the Military Intelligence Service, MIS, the secret unit that translated and interpreted for Allied forces in the Pacific, but ended up serving with Love Company of the 442nd.

"In the 442nd, you had a lot of friends," Kizuka said. "We fought as a team in Europe. The MIS guys worked alone."

Teamwork would be required of the Nisei in April 1945 as they moved into position to assault the Gothic Line — German defensive fortifications that had halted the Allied advance in Italy for five months. Kizuka and his unit were to attack a strongpoint, Mount Folgorito, from the rear; a risky plan that required a stealthy eight-hour climb in the black of night up a narrow, nearly vertical mountain trail. Enemy soldiers were asleep or eating breakfast and totally surprised when the Nisei attacked shortly after daybreak.

"If they were awake, I don't think I would be here to tell you this story," he confided. The Nisei broke the Gothic Line in 32 minutes.

Kizuka was wounded on April 19, 1945, and another man killed, just before the war ended in Europe.

"The man that got killed when I later got wounded? I didn't even know his name," he said.

Kizuka was afraid his friends would sail home without him. He sneaked out of the hospital and rejoined his unit, which, instead of going home, got orders for six months of occupation duty in Italy.

Compared to combat, where they "bathed out of their helmets or in rivers," the occupation turned out to be pleasant duty. German POWs would work for the GIs, shining boots, doing laundry and waiting tables. Kizuka said the Army used the campus of the University of Florence to hold refresher courses for GIs who, like himself, would soon be returning to college back in the States.

In recent years, Kizuka has been asked about the tough missions that the Nisei were given.

"Was the 442nd abused or were they the best outfit to do the job? A little of both," he said.

The Purple Heart, the Bronze Star and his other medals and citations well attest to the service of the young man from Love Company.

"It was my duty," he said. "I did what I had to do."

Hiroshi Kaku

"I had to volunteer for the 442nd just to get out of Lanai."

Hiroshi Kaku returned to his dining room table after retrieving his old Army uniform jacket from a nearby closet. It was pressed and ready, boasting commendation ribbons on the chest, master sergeant's stripes on one sleeve and the 442nd patch on the opposite shoulder. The jacket still fit, he said.

He took his seat in front of a plate of sweets and a cup of green tea that he had not touched in the hour he had been telling of his World War II enlistment and a career in the Army.

"When the war broke out, I was in Lanai, growing pineapple. Martial law was declared, we couldn't leave the house at night and there was no civilian transportation between the islands for the rest of the war," said Kaku, whose big family was in Hilo, on the Big Island, where his father ran a tofu factory. "I was stuck there for two years until FDR decided to let Japanese Americans into the military in March '43. I had to volunteer for the 442nd just to get out of Lanai.

"My older brother Haruo was drafted before the war. He was at Schofield Barracks, and they took the rifles away from Japanese Americans and had them doing menial labor after Pearl Harbor. He joined the 100th Battalion and went to Camp McCoy for training while I was training at Camp Shelby. The 100th came to Louisiana for maneuvers, and that was the first time I saw him in three years. The next time would be on the road in Italy, when the 100th joined with the 442nd in Cittaveccia. In the Vosges Mountains, he had trench foot so bad they sent him back to the States and then to Hawaii for a medical discharge. He was a rifleman in Charlie Company, and I was in Anti-tank Company.

"They needed anti-tank for the invasion of Southern France. We were the only company to be detached from the 442nd," Kaku said.

"We flew in on gliders to support the 517th Airborne Regiment, part of the 1st Airborne Task Force. The gliders were only made of aluminum tubing and canvas with plywood floors, and our guns were too large to fit, so we trained on smaller, lighter British guns that used the same ammunition. We trained for two weeks just on properly strapping down our guns, trailers and jeeps in the gliders. The only thing that didn't go airborne with us was the mess hall! We had two training flights. They took us to a small airport near Rome

and locked us up until we took off — it was top secret, and they didn't want word of the invasion getting out," he remembers.

"Each plane pulls two gliders, and they tow them on nylon rope about this big," Kaku said, touching his index finger to his thumb. "The nylon stretches out, and the takeoff is so smooth you don't even feel it."

As with paratroop drops, the Allies rarely employed gliders to deliver invasion troops, as both operations were notoriously dangerous and chaotic. Men dangling from parachutes might land over a wide area; lacking their own propulsion, glider pilots had limited choices of safe landing areas. In addition to fences, rocks, and trees, the Germans had erected telephone poles over vast areas of level ground where gliders might land. A tree or telephone pole would tear a glider apart, certainly killing its two-man crew up front and killing or injuring troops riding in the back.

"From the air we could look down and see the landing craft going in to the beach. The 517th was already there. They had landed at night and cut down as many poles as possible, but they could not cut them all down," Kaku said. "There were many casualties during the landing. Hitting a single phone line would flip a glider, and many ran into trees when they landed. We got lucky — we ran into a high road bank, and it stopped us.

"The troops that landed on the beaches moved north, and we moved east. We had very little resistance. We were lucky. We ran into no tanks whatsoever."

He pointed to a tiny medal pin on the European Campaign ribbon adorning his uniform.

"We were the only Nisei unit to get the Arrowhead pin, indicating we took part in an invasion," he explained. "We stuck with the 517th all the way to the Italian border. That's when the 442nd went to France. We left the British guns with the paratroops, got our old guns and met the 442nd in Bruyères. The 517th was relieved at the same time. Later, they dropped into Holland and got really beaten up.

"After the war, they sent me back to Hawaii. I looked for work but could not find a decent job. The Army said if I re-enlisted, I could hold my rank and pick my assignment, so I did, and I requested assignment to Japan.

"At that time, all Japanese Americans going to Japan had to go to ATIS, Allied Translator and Interpreter Section. If they

were qualified in Japanese, they would keep them there, since they were desperate for linguists. My Japanese was not very good. Because I had a background in photography, I was assigned to the photo section of G-2, Military Intelligence."

Kaku served in Japan as a lab technician and still photographer from 1947–1951, with assignments to Korea and Taiwan, then called Formosa. In addition to the black and white motion picture and photo films he processed, there was plenty of microfilm of captured documents, all to be translated by linguists, many of them Japanese nationals working for the American forces. Constance, a diplomat's daughter, was one of them, and she and Kaku were married in 1950.

Kaku's longest, and last, assignment was to the Army Pictorial Center in Long Island City, New York, the Army's principal filmmaking facility. He retired in 1965 and opened his own photography business in Manhattan, working for big advertising companies.

The 442nd held its first reunion in Chicago in 1959, Kaku remembers. At first, reunions were held every two years, then every three years, then every five, alternating between the Mainland and Hawaii. The 65th reunion was held in 2008. The 70th will be in Honolulu in 2013. Kaku has attended them all.

Shig Doi

"They handed us a rifle and said, 'You are an infantryman.'"

The small home sits in the country, maybe a mile from San Pablo Bay, north of San Francisco. A railroad runs through large grass-covered parcels and past scrap metal recyclers and derelict greenhouses. A hero lives here.

Shig Doi, 93, waits in the sun by his front door. As he looks across the street, he remembers a different landscape.

"This was all greenhouses at one time," he said. "Now the flowers come from South America, where they don't have to heat the greenhouses like they do here. The local guys couldn't compete any longer."

Doi padded back to his recliner in his stocking feet. He was watching golf on television, hoping Tiger would win something. It was Sunday, and his wife Yoshiko ducked out the back door on her way to church.

"Before the war, everything was anti-Japanese. They hung a big sign on the Bay Bridge, 'Boycott Jap Goods.' We had 85 acres of diversified fruit trees — pear, peach, persimmon, plus 20 acres of grapes.

"But Placer County was very racist. It's always been that way. My folks were among the first released from camp; they still had the farm and they wanted to go back home. Then the place got shot at, fire bombed, dynamited. They caught the guys and tried them, but even the trial was fixed, and they got off."

Two of the three men were soldiers. The defense attorney said, "This is a white man's country," and local residents donated to a defense fund for the accused.

"Jury Acquits Three Arsonists in Sumio Doi Case," a headline read.

Doi was in the last group of draftees before Nisei were given 4-C status after Pearl Harbor. Japanese American soldiers at West Coast installations were relieved of their weapons and transferred to bases in the Midwest.

"I went through basic medical training at Camp Grant, Illinois. In the first part of 1942, I moved up to the station hospital and ended up in the dental department," Doi said. "Then they threw us out.

"Our top administrators at the station hospital were all Nisei. The Army needed replacements for the 442nd. They scoured the 10 relocation camps but they didn't get enough volunteers. Hell, they said, we have all these guys in the Midwest, and anyone with a Japanese surname was sent to Camp Blanding, Florida,

or McClelland, Alabama. This was in early '44. They handed us a rifle and said, 'You are an infantryman.' I was a T/4, but they busted me down to corporal — we all got busted — one rifleman was a licensed pharmacist. He would have been much more valuable in another job. He was the first guy killed the first day in the push for Bruyères. But that's how the Army does things!

"This was the second basic training for us, maybe the third for some guys. We had training like no one else — 16 weeks. We trained on every weapon from the .45 pistol up to anti-tank 57 mm. We were replacements, to go wherever we were needed, and we were trained so we could take over any position. I was trained with a B.A.R., a Browning Automatic Rifle, but as an infantryman, I could pick up any weapon on the battlefield and know how to use it."

Doi said the replacements were consolidated at Camp Shelby before shipping overseas to meet the 442nd in the fall of 1944.

"Fighting in the Vosges, if you advanced 100 or 200 yards a day it was an accomplishment. You didn't know where you were going. It was black as night under those trees, all this big around," he said, holding out his arms to demonstrate. "Once, we got lost and ended up in No Man's Land. Luckily, we saw the Germans first. The most dreaded 88 shell is coming into our perimeter continuously. Shuji Taketomo, the radioman who just passed away, told me one day he counted 85 shells come in.

"At the Lost Battalion, I, K and L Companies were in that sector. I was in the patrol that made contact with the Lost Battalion. Tak Senzaki was the squad leader. We were a pick-up squad — no one knew each other — just ragtag soldiers that formed a squad. What burns me is they ordered us forward again after we broke through to the Lost Battalion. Any other unit that had done what we did would have been pulled back, told 'good job,' and given a rest. But because of our sacrifice, we got them out.

"General Dahlquist, he bled us. Every day I was making two combat patrols, and on every one we lost a man. He bled us down to nothing. He finally relieved us when we had nothing left. I Company had just eight riflemen of 185. We stood in formation and the general said, 'Where are all the men?' and Colonel Miller said, 'This is all that are left.'"

Shig's memories of combat brought up another subject, medical care for veterans.

"I can understand the soldiers from Iraq and Afghanistan. The V.A. doctors are not combat doctors. They don't know the fear and how you feel all over. If you have a doctor who has been under fire, he'll understand what the enlisted man is trying to tell him. I've been shot at, blown unconscious and bleeding from my nose and ears, lost my hearing in one ear because of a grenade, and that doesn't mean a damn. You need doctors and interviewers who can understand," Shig said. "I have fallen down many times for no reason, but you tell the doctor and he gives you a pill — and that's it.

"What gets me, the war is almost over, and on the last patrol a machine gun opens up and kills the new radioman. My friend in I Company headquarters, he got killed in the last days when the HQ got blown up. The night before, a 'short round' hit a tree and killed a platoon sergeant. Nothing is more demoralizing than to see your men get hit by friendly fire, and there were lots of casualties from friendly fire.

"My younger brother Carl was drafted into the MIS in '43, and Sumio, my older brother, was running the farm. When you have three sons and two are already in the service, the third doesn't have to go, but they drafted Sumio at the end of the war. I requested an early discharge to get home and help my parents, but the local Red Cross said my parents weren't having any problems at all. That's how racist they were back home. In fact, when my friend Shig Yokote and I were drafted, 23 or so of the 30 guys drafted were Nisei. That was the local draft board. But to this day I remember my elementary school principal, Mr. Welch, came to the train and shook our hands when we went off to the service. He didn't have to do that. Little things like that really count in your life. It stuck with me. You remember it for a lifetime.

"When the 442nd was going home, I was a tech sergeant, and I left Naples with a group of 30 men. We took the *Mariposa* across the ocean, seven days, flat on my back, seasick as a dog. We separated at Camp Kilmer, New Jersey — I took one plane, and they took another. I landed in Sacramento, and I heard something on the P.A. about a plane crashing, but, thinking about the farm and wanting to get discharged, I forgot about it. I got discharged at Camp Beale, in Marysville, and they give me $1.25 travel money, so I hitchhiked home. My ride lets me off at a gas station and there was no sweetheart, no crowds, no

parents to welcome me. A man standing there says. 'Helluva way to get home, huh?'

"I had to work the next day, since Sumio had been drafted. My mother told me a plane had crashed six miles away on a neighbor's farm. It was the plane with the rest of my guys. And what really burns me, our neighbor said the fire department came out and there are all these injured guys lying around, but they refused to help them because they were Japanese American."

Shig agreed to work the farm for one year, and then he moved to San Francisco to look for a job.

"I walked that Market Street looking for a job, any job, and I hit a blank wall. I tried the State Health Department. They didn't ask about my qualifications. They asked if I was in 'that Japanese American unit.' I said yes, and they hired me. That became my password: Go For Broke. We broke the barriers."

Yoshiko returned from church, smiled, and began preparing lunch. The golf tournament had ended, and maybe church was on Shig's mind.

"I feel I must have had the Man walking right beside me," he said. "I could have been on that plane that crashed. You might start digging a foxhole and then decide to move it 10 or 15 feet, and later a shell comes in where you started digging. Sometimes the man right next to me would get hit, but I didn't even get a Purple Heart.

"I don't have any friends left," he said. "I've lost four friends in the last month."

He showed the citations for his two Bronze Stars, one from combat in France, the other, Italy.

"They don't mean a thing," he said. "I had my day in the Army. One day you laugh. Another day you cry."

Kelly Yeiichi Kuwayama

"Right and left of you, people are being shot and killed."

Kelly Yeiichi Kuwayama stood in his cool living room holding a letter from the French ambassador, on a typically hot and humid summer day in Washington, D.C. The letter named him Knight of the Legion of Honor, France's most prestigious award. It was the latest in a series of honors for Kuwayama, a medic with the 442nd Regimental Combat Team. The Silver Star, the Italian Croce di Valore — the medals seem to find him. He certainly didn't seek them out, especially the Purple Heart.

He grew up in New York City where his father ran an import-export food business, an art goods store and a Japanese restaurant on the Upper East Side, in a neighborhood with Irish cops and plumbers, Czechs and Germans.

"The East Coast was all immigrants," he said.

During the 1905 Russo-Japanese War, his father dressed himself as a Japanese soldier and sold American and Japanese flags and trinkets on the boardwalk in Atlantic City.

"It was the most profitable business up to that time he ever had."

His father made some money in the stock market and returned to Japan to find a wife. The market crashed just as his bride arrived from Japan.

Kuwayama graduated from Princeton University in 1940, one of only two Japanese American students on campus, and went to work for the Japanese Chamber of Commerce. Older than the average Nisei veteran, he was drafted almost a year before Pearl Harbor, in January 1941. In his tent, five of the eight men were college graduates, and one was already an architect.

The men were issued World War I uniforms and, instead of basic training, sent directly to various units. Kuwayama was assigned to Fort Hancock, New York, ostensibly to direct fire for a National Guard coast artillery battery guarding the New York harbor. A general came around and asked his name. The next day he was transferred away from the battery and, soon, away from the coast. He was reassigned to Madison Barracks, an old Army post in Watertown, New York, near the Canadian border.

After Pearl Harbor, he moved to the medical unit at Fort Ethan Allen, Vermont, and by the time he volunteered for the 442nd in 1943, he was a surgical technician and a sergeant. He discovered the Nisei did things a bit differently.

"The first thing I noticed was that rice was eaten three times a day at Camp Shelby," he said.

At reunions, Kuwayama is singled out as one of the veterans' heroes.

"Kelly and the other medics kept us going. They saved our lives many times. Several got killed," one veteran said. "We had our rifles. They had a helmet with a red cross on it."

Kuwayama said he didn't even have that.

"A helmet with a red cross on it would have given away our whereabouts. I did carry a small Red Cross flag when I went out into No Man's Land."

After aiding the wounded during the battle for the Lost Battalion, Kuwayama was wounded himself. Quiet and humble, he shrugged off the notion of bravery but remembered the horrors of combat.

"It was very gray and rainy. The fighting was fierce — right and left of you, people are being shot and killed. Rifle companies of 200 or so men were reduced to 12. When the fighting was in Italy, the Germans would shoot three rounds with an 88, kill a couple of guys, and we would shoot back with 155 mm guns for an hour. It was terrible arithmetic."

His wounds were treated at Plombières-les-Bains hospital and he returned to the front lines after a few weeks, "more or less recovered," rejoining the company in the Maritime Alps. Upon Germany's surrender, Kuwayama was among the first to go home on the points system. He had nearly five years in the Army, a Silver Star and Purple Heart. He was shipped to Fort Dix, New Jersey, where his processing took only a few days before he was back in New York City, a civilian.

Kuwayama attended Harvard Business School under the GI Bill, earned his MBA and sent hundreds of letters to Wall Street firms looking for work. He finally was hired as statistician for Western Electric. He was later recruited for the New York office of Nomura Securities.

"Japanese firms were known for not promoting local hires, and I accepted the offer, provided it included possibilities for promotion. That meant I would have to work for a year in Japan under the same conditions for my age and experience as any Japanese employee."

He moved to Japan in 1951, at a time when the country had become a base for the fighting in Korea, and American, British, Dutch and French companies were actively investing and trying to re-establish themselves after the war.

As promised, the company soon promoted him, and he served as their general manager in New York City. He later worked in Washington, D.C., for the Office of Foreign Direct Investments and at the Securities and Exchange Commission, retiring in 1984.

Kuwayama's Knight of the Legion of Honor medal was presented at a grand ceremony at Arromanches, on France's Normandy coast, with representatives of the French, American and other Allied governments honoring the soldiers who fought for the liberation of Europe.

For the first time, he saw the long rows of white crosses filling the big American cemetery behind Omaha Beach. It is something he will never forget.

"It was a heart-wrenching and stirring sight to see."

Jaxson Ono   442nd Regimental Combat Team   World War II

Don Seki   442nd Regimental Combat Team   World War II

Shuji Taketomo   442nd Regimental Combat Team   World War II

Mum Arii 442nd Regimental Combat Team World War II

Harry Akune   Military Intelligence Service   World War II

Nelson Akagi   522nd Field Artillery Battalion   World War II

Jimmie Kanaya   442nd Regimental Combat Team   WWII   Korea   Vietnam

George Akita   Military Intelligence Service   World War II

Masaji Mike Tsuji   442nd Regimental Combat Team   World War II

Royal Manaka 100th Infantry Battalion World War II

Jim Tanaka   442nd Regimental Combat Team   World War II

Harry Kawamura   442nd Regimental Combat Team   WWII   Korea   Vietnam

The War Ends ... Then Korea

Hostilities ended in Europe on May 8, 1945, and the 442nd halted its push against the Germans and began the task of disarming and guarding large numbers of prisoners of war. Its detached 522nd Field Artillery Battalion was in Munich after liberating prisoners at Dachau. Some American soldiers began leaving for home, based on a points system that counted months in service, commendations and number of children, among other factors.

But fighting was still going on in the Pacific. Men and supplies were being readied for the invasion of Japan, and members of the 442nd knew days of uncertainty that only ended with Japan's surrender August 15 after atomic bombs struck Hiroshima and Nagasaki.

MISers joined teams on the ground surveying the A-bomb damage. They found flattened cities, dead and wounded civilians, and their own family members, displaced and sometimes suffering from radiation sickness. Harry Fukuhara found his family just before his mother died. Others found brothers and cousins, conscripts in the Imperial armed forces, weak, emotionally devastated, and sometimes bitter toward their victorious American relatives.

United States Gen. Douglas MacArthur, Supreme Commander for the Allied Powers, moved his headquarters to Tokyo as the Americans disarmed the Japanese military, aided the starving population and began to establish a new government. Thousands of enemy soldiers returned to Japan from China, Korea and Manchuria and were debriefed by the MIS as American forces began seeking intelligence on China and Russia, adversaries in the new Cold War. There was also the task of identifying, arresting and trying war criminals, which required linguists for investigative, prosecution and defense teams.

MISers were recruited for reenlistment with proffered promotions to officer. Some stayed in the service; others were happy to get out of the Army and get home to help their families.

West Coast veterans returned home to chaotic lives. Japan-towns were unrecognizable to those who knew them before the war. Neighbors or friends may have looked after their property, but it was just as often stripped bare. One successful Issei farmer returned to find his equipment picked over, leaving him with a single old tractor. His neighbors were silent.

Nisei veterans signed up for their GI benefits. Some began or resumed college study. Others took on the task of rebuilding a family farm or business. Families needed housing, but legal covenants dictated where they might or might not live. Jobs were few, especially for those with Japanese faces. Attitudes had not changed. President Truman ordered the armed forces integrated in 1948, but veterans were turned down for membership in the American Legion, VFW and the Lions Club. Soldiers still in uniform were denied haircuts and restaurant meals. Hawaii veterans had to start their own bank, as others would not lend to them. The veterans' Issei parents could not apply for citizenship until 1952.

Few 442nd soldiers chose to reenlist, having had enough of the Army, enough of war. Some ran past Army recruiters at the discharge centers. Most had been in the Army two or three years, but for those drafted before Pearl Harbor, it might be five years or more. Wives and sweethearts waited at home, the Hawaiians longed for the Islands, Mainlanders were anxious to reunite with their families and reestablish a normal life after Internment. Wounds ached to be healed.

Some men joined the Army Reserve. Times were tough, and they were happy for a little extra income. Hiroshi Miyamura, reluctant at first to join up, remembers the recruiter's pitch.

"There's little chance the U.S. will be going to war again, but if we did, you'd want to help your country and join up, wouldn't you?"

Within five years, the bullets would fly again.

When war broke out on the Korean Peninsula on June 25, 1950, MIS linguists were in demand once again. Japan had occupied Korea for 35 years, and maps and documents created during that time were all in Japanese. The Japanese defeat left a power vacuum Communists and others were eager to fill. MISers transitioned to full-fledged intelligence agents, operating against individuals and groups seeking to subvert the fledgling South Korean government.

Korea was as unknown to Americans in 1950 as Pearl Harbor had been in 1941. Men too young for World War II were drafted to fight in Korea, including some of the Nisei veterans' younger brothers. The 442nd's reputation was well known to American commanders and they expected Japanese Americans to reprise the Go For Broke motto and fight like hell.

Korea has been called "The Forgotten War." For those who fought there, it will not be forgotten. It was the same hell as any war.

Daniel K. Inouye

"To be honored by your brothers is the highest honor."

United States Senator Daniel K. Inouye gazed from the podium at the ballroom filled with constituents and fellow veterans, many his friends. He stood stolidly, unselfconscious of the slack right sleeve that hung at his side. Perhaps taking measure of himself and his accomplishments, he waited for the applause to die down, while the words of introduction summarizing his career echoed across the room and, perhaps, in his mind:

Elected to the Hawaii Territorial Legislature in 1954.
United States Senator from Hawaii for nine terms.
Member of the Senate Appropriations Committee.
Keynote Speaker of the 1968 Democratic
    National Convention.
Member of the Senate Watergate Committee.
Chairman of the Senate "Iran-Contra" Hearings.

Applause filled the room.

Standing before his friends at the reunion, it seemed impossible more than 60 years had passed since he was a 20-year-old, just one of the boys of the 442nd. Recognized early as a leader and awarded a battlefield commission, he would distinguish himself again and again on the battlefields of France and Italy, be severely wounded — indeed, lose an arm in the last days of the war — and earn over a dozen commendations, including the Medal of Honor. In 2011, he spoke in Washington at the Congressional Gold Medal events, joining other veterans as they received the nation's highest honor.

He spent 20 months recovering in Army hospitals. In a hospital in Battle Creek, Michigan, Inouye befriended a soldier wounded on a neighboring hill in Italy with whom he would later serve in the U.S. Senate, Bob Dole of Kansas. The two men were wounded within days of each other. They began a decades-long friendship that trumped their politics. Dole, a Republican, ran for president in 1996 and retired from the Senate. Inouye, a Democrat, continues to serve as the nation's senior senator.

"Dan is one of us," Dole later said of his old friend. "The guy you'd want in a foxhole with you."

Inouye credits Dole with starting him on a public service career after the severe wounds derailed his longtime plans of becoming a doctor. As bombs fell on Pearl Harbor, Inouye,

a high school student, volunteering with the Red Cross, not returning to his home for several days. As soon as Japanese Americans were allowed to enlist, he ended his medical studies and joined the 442nd.

Inouye's Easy Company buddies refer to him as "Senator Dan," a friendly moniker that keeps him humble in their presence. ("We donate to Dan's campaigns, which is funny, because most of us are Republicans," one Mainland veteran confided.) No matter his accomplishments in Washington, he shared their youthful experiences: the modest upbringing, the Hawaiian cane fields and mom-and-pop stores, the suspicion and hatred following Pearl Harbor, the baggy GI uniforms that hung on the small-framed Nisei, the welcome but infrequent appearances of shower trucks with hot water, and the Red Cross girls with coffee and doughnuts.

"Reunion," he began, his mellifluous baritone at once calming and evoking. "We gather because we want to recall the past, our youth and the good times. All of us recall the past, but we recollect with different eyes.

"Support, inspiration, values we learned from our parents," he continued, weaving a familiar and inspirational tableau of the Nisei experience. Like most veterans, he spoke more of the good times than of the bad. He did not mention his own wounds, but recalled the fierce fighting in France.

"I don't remember the Lost Battalion," he confessed. "In fact, I don't want to remember it."

Those seated near the podium could see the senator touch the gold star that hung on a sky-blue ribbon around his neck, first placed there by President Clinton when he awarded new, upgraded medals to Nisei veterans at the White House in June 2000.

"As a politician, I have been honored many times. But to be honored by your brothers is the highest honor," Inouye said.

"When I wear this medal, I wear it on your behalf. There is no such thing as a one-man hero. I can think of at least a dozen men in my company who should be wearing this.

"The medals belong to you."

George R. Ariyoshi

"Today affects tomorrow."

War in the Pacific reached its bloody zenith in 1945 with the invasions of Iwo Jima and Okinawa, the firebombing of Japanese cities and the horror of two atomic bombs.

During the war, Hawaii had evolved from an isolated mid-ocean outpost to America's military headquarters in the Pacific. The islands prospered with the wartime injection of personnel and dollars; it was a paradise, but an imperfect one. During the war, military authority ruled the islands. Not yet a state, the territory's governor and judges were appointed by Washington, instead of elected by its people. That system continued until 1959, when Hawaii became the 50th state.

Until then, "We had no say," explained former Hawaii Governor George R. Ariyoshi, taking in the view of Honolulu from a corporate conference room high above the city.

A young man in uniform, Ariyoshi left the islands for the first time in August 1945 aboard a troopship carrying him to basic training on the Mainland. He was miserably seasick the entire voyage to Angel Island in San Francisco Bay, where the recruits transferred to a train for the long trip to Camp Hood — now Fort Hood — Texas. Before their training was complete, Ariyoshi was singled out and sent to Military Intelligence Service Language School at Fort Snelling, Minnesota, destined to become one of the youngest MIS soldiers.

Upon graduating the language school, the young linguist sailed on another ship in August 1946, this one to Japan.

"The Emperor, on a visit to MacArthur, said, 'You can do what you want with me, but save our people,'" Ariyoshi said. "Japan could have been divided, like Germany, but they weren't. The Japanese, the older ones involved in the post-war recovery, understand that. The U.S. and MacArthur wanted Japan to recover economically as soon as possible. We could not occupy Japan forever, and we wanted them to come back as our friend, not our enemy. You can defeat an enemy and return a defeated nation not to enemy status, but to a friendly nation in tune with our own thinking."

Intent on becoming a lawyer, Ariyoshi turned down reenlistment when his tour ended. He was anxious to resume his studies and make up for lost time. His father, Ryozo, who left Japan with only a third-grade education, taught his son the value of education.

"'Hadaka ni nattemo. Even if I have to go naked, I will make it possible for you to become a lawyer,' he told me."

The future governor graduated from University of Michigan Law School in 1952.

Governor Ariyoshi's career shifted to politics in 1954 when John A. "Jack" Burns, a Democratic leader, urged him to run for the Territorial House of Representatives. Ariyoshi won in a landmark election — the first time Democrats gained control of the territory's legislature. In 1970, then-Governor Burns asked him to run as his lieutenant governor.

"After 16 years in the legislature, I had begun thinking about retirement, but Jack Burns was worried about 1974, and who would succeed him," Ariyoshi recalled. "He said, 'Listen, no person other than white men has ever been elected governor. No one born in Hawaii has ever been elected governor. This will continue unless you break the chain. The people need to understand they can succeed.'"

Ariyoshi was elected lieutenant governor and went on to become America's first non-white governor, leading Hawaii for 13 years, 1974–86.

"In 1974, Vietnam was still raging, and people became more open about speaking out. I spent a lot of time talking to people. I wanted all people to express their views, to put it all on the table. One should never be afraid of controversy; it's an opportunity to learn from others and to teach others — a two-way street.

"When I became governor, I was concerned about our rapid growth; Hawaii's population was growing at three times the U.S. rate. I spent much time thinking about the future: job creation, housing, education, transportation. What did Hawaii want to be in 20 or 30 years? What is our preferred future? Today affects tomorrow," he said.

"I don't speak much about my time in the MIS. Those who served earlier did the important work. The MIS were not just decoding Japanese, they could understand the Japanese culture — not just the plan, but the spirit of the enemy. This allowed us to meet the enemy and be successful.

"I am very grateful for the MIS men who preceded me, and for the 442nd and 100th Infantry, for what they did. I made a promise to myself that I would take up where they left off on the battlefield. I took their example and started my work when I got home. I had the burden of doing the best I could do for Hawaii."

Kiyo Sato

"Five brothers and I served during World War II and the Korean War."

The book is wonderful, a revelation of unconquerable human spirit that survived one of America's greatest mistakes and embarrassments. *Kiyo's Story* is just that, the story of Kiyo Sato as a young woman, a product of the Depression, an internee, nurse, veteran, public health professional, inventor, lecturer and writer.

The eighty-some-year-old author sat in her living room, a doorway removed from her office (not her writing office — that is a Formica table in a doughnut shop across town).

"Most of my book is about my family," the author modestly began the conversation. "Even during the Depression, we were OK. We always had plenty of vegetables to eat. I even took piano lessons for 75 cents an hour," she said.

The oldest of nine, Kiyo held the job of mother's helper, wrangling her brothers and sisters to meals, chores and school. The days following Pearl Harbor brought big changes to the family. Japanese Americans were forbidden to travel from dark to dawn, or more than five miles from their homes. The euphemistic "evacuation" began when she was 19 years old.

"This was my first year in college, and I had such high hopes," she said. "We were sent to the Pinedale Assembly Center with 5,000 other people for two and a half months, then to Poston, Arizona. There, they drove us the 17 miles into the desert in an Army truck. It was 127 degrees! I passed out. At Poston, 18,000 people were interned in three camps. We tried to joke about it, and we named them Poston, Toast 'em and Roast 'em."

Japanese Americans were allowed to leave internment for schools and jobs outside the exclusion zone. Kiyo soon left Poston for Hillsdale College in Michigan. Her brother, Steve Seiji Sato, joined the 442nd, but a Navy recruiter turned down Kiyo's 1944 request for enlistment. The Air Force accepted her when she volunteered again in 1951 during the Korean War.

"By then, I was already a nurse," she said proudly, adding, "Five brothers and I served during World War II and the Korean War."

She requested an overseas assignment, and two months later, she was assigned to Clark Air Force Base in the Philippines, then soon to the big airbase at Tachikawa, Japan. She recalls that winter in Japan, and a single *ume-no-ki*, a white flowering plum tree blossoming in the snow at the hospital.

"Every day, it was only my footprints which went to that tree. That memory forever thrills me."

She returned to Sacramento after a two-year enlistment, working for the public health service, and later as a school nurse. She served families in rural Sacramento County, traveling the same farm roads she did while growing up before World War II. While undertaking the vision and hearing testing of hundreds of 3- and 4-year-olds, she found existing tests didn't work for young children. She invented the Blackbird Vision Screening method, which allowed children as young as pre-school to identify bird silhouettes instead of letters of the alphabet.

Kiyo's childhood dream was not nursing, but journalism. When she was whisked from her home and imprisoned, she guarded her journals above all else. Her observations and thoughts on the struggles of a farm family during the Depression, her journey to adulthood and the uncertainty and humiliation of internment, honed by the perspective of her years, make for a powerful volume. Each morning, she dutifully writes for several hours in the accommodating doughnut shop. It took 60 years of journaling to finish her book.

"If I wrote it when I was 40, I don't think it would be a very interesting book," she confided. "But when I hit 80, I thought I'd better get going!"

She and other members of her VFW Post speak to schools — from primary grades to universities — on what she calls "lessons of our lifetime." The speakers' bureau began in 1975 with 15 vigorous individuals, she said. Now, only Kiyo and one or two others are still able to participate.

"I ask kids what they would pack if they were only allowed one suitcase, like we were. They say: family photos, underwear, flashlights, even video games. Then I tell them what my father brought with us: a hammer, saw, nails, baling wire, a bucket, a big tarp. We got to camp, and he built shelves and a table for my mother. We could hang things on nails. The big tarp, wetted and hung from the ceiling, became our air conditioner. We didn't have running water, so we fetched water in the bucket. Thinking back, it seems everyone in our block asked to borrow that hammer and saw!

"My father was a great storyteller," she said, "And I've talked to schools ever since I left camp."

She paused.

"I've never had a chance to forget."

Shigeo Iwamasa

"After Pearl Harbor we were 'Damn Japs.'"

"Today we are friends, but right after Pearl Harbor we were 'Damn Japs,'" Shigeo Iwamasa sadly remembers.

Like all Hawaiians, Iwamasa's life changed forever on December 7th, 1941. He volunteered for the 442nd as soon as the call went out. Like many recruits from the Hawaiian plantations, he was so thin he gained weight in boot camp.

"The only parts of my uniform that fit were the cap, tie, belt and handkerchief," he said.

The diminutive and soft-spoken veteran seemed almost too gentle to be an infantryman, but like the other 442nd soldiers, he carried the heavy M1 Garand rifle in combat, and he learned to fight and to survive on the Italian and French hillsides, and later, in Korea.

"The cardinal sin in combat is bunching up — one shot could kill all of you. Most of combat is dull, just waiting around. The shooting only lasts for a half-hour or sometimes only a few minutes, but the night before, you can't sleep. You'd try to have a hot meal. You didn't know if you would see your friends again."

In Europe, Shigeo could not tolerate the C-rations the troops were issued. He found better fare among the canned German meals he picked up on the battlefield — meat, potatoes and cabbage. The slender rifleman discarded his bulky gas mask and filled its case with his German rations — and extra clips for his M1.

"You needed those," he said.

While the 442nd prepared to leave France for Italy, he was assigned to the 121st Quartermaster Car Company, to later become a staff driver for officers at the Potsdam Conference. When the war ended, he drove into Berlin to see the few sights remaining: the Reichstag, the Brandenburg Gate, the Reich Chancellery and the Olympic Stadium. There was little else still standing.

Iwamasa was discharged in December 1945 and re-enlisted in 1948. He was stationed at Fort Ruger, Hawaii, when bodies of the 442nd men began coming back from temporary graves in Europe for burial at Punchbowl National Cemetery. His unit conducted two burial ceremonies in the morning; had lunch; showered and changed into fresh uniforms; and held two more burials in the afternoon — an emotional routine he and the other soldiers struggled to maintain. Shig remembers serving in the honor guard for Ernie Pyle, the popular news correspondent who was killed on the tiny island of Ie Jima, near Okinawa, and buried at Punchbowl.

When war in Korea broke out, he was with the 5th Infantry Regiment at Schofield Barracks and was soon en route to Pusan and the fighting there. He caught pneumonia in the field, staying on the line for another 10 days before being sent to a hospital and eventually to Japan. After Korea, Iwamasa went to school on the GI Bill and worked for Northrop Aircraft Co. in California for over 30 years.

Today, he lives on Maui and enjoys visiting old friends on the Mainland and attending 442nd reunions.

"The most satisfying thing is to see the men at the reunions," Shig said. "They survived."

George Fujikawa

"We fired our rifles to zero them in, threw one grenade and left for Korea."

Orchids filled the house and yard. Any free space, it seemed, was filled with pots of green topped with gold flowers. George Fujikawa confessed to being the gardener.

"I grew up on a farm, so I always had that in me, I guess."

Fujikawa grew up around Isleton, California, where his family moved from one leased plot to another growing pears, corn, melons and tomatoes. He was 11 when the family relocated to the internment camp at Heart Mountain, a few miles east of Cody, Wyoming. It was tight quarters, and eight children still lived at home.

At camp, there were kids all around.

"For me, camp was fun — it was hard on my parents and older brothers and sisters. My parents never talked about camp, never complained."

He joined the Boy Scouts. The Scouts restricted their activities to within the camp, except for one memorable trip in the summer of 1944, when they spent a week in Yellowstone National Park building a bridge over Nez Perce Creek. The bridge is still there, Fujikawa says, but no longer in use.

The war ended. In less than a year they moved to San Francisco, and soon, on to nearby Centerville. From school to school, Fujikawa still found prejudice against Japanese Americans. High school counselors did not encourage further education for Nisei. Maybe because of this, Fujikawa joined the Army in 1948 and finished his studies at McKinley High School while stationed in Honolulu.

Fresh out of basic training, Fujikawa spent six months on Eniwetok, a mile-long strip of sand a few miles from the atomic bomb test site in the Pacific.

"It was very secretive: no cameras allowed and we could not write about it in letters home. 'We're doing fine' is about all we could say. After I left, they tested the hydrogen bomb there, and some of the guys later said the island was gone."

He was working in an Army warehouse in Honolulu when the Korean War broke out.

"The Army was at skeleton strength. They asked for volunteers, and six from my company signed up. We fired our rifles to zero them in, threw one grenade and left for Korea. We landed in Pusan and the second day we went into combat on the Pusan Perimeter."

His unit, the 5th Regimental Combat Team, replaced an infantry regiment that had been devastated in the early fighting.

K Company, hastily formed and under strength, consisted of three squads of nine men each, instead of the usual four squads of 12 men. After a month, they were assigned an additional squad of South Korean soldiers, Fujikawa said.

The 5th RCT had many veterans of the heroic 442nd, but not K Company, which was composed mostly of men enlisting after World War II.

"But the white officers expected us to fight like the 442nd," Fujikawa remembers.

The 1st and 2nd Battalions of the 5th RCT spearheaded a breakout of the Pusan Perimeter and later advanced to within 16 miles of the Yalu River, the border with China. The enemy preferred to fight at night, hiding during daylight hours when U.S. Navy and Air Force planes ruled the skies and battlefield. One day Fujikawa received his McKinley High School diploma in the mail. Chinese soldiers attacked his unit that night. The Americans retreated, leaving their belongings behind. Fujikawa lost his diploma.

The 3rd Battalion held a hilltop, surrounded by the enemy and in danger of being overrun, but the Chinese instead went after the 1st and 2nd Battalions, wiping them out. The American regimental commander was relieved of duty for losing so many men. Fujikawa, a squad leader, was wounded by a grenade and evacuated to Japan, then to Hawaii, and finally to the mainland. He had been in Korea seven months. He spent six months hospitalized and another six on temporary duty.

His brother, Kenji, was drafted during the Korean War and served at Fort Lewis, Washington.

"We never talked much about the Korean War. People didn't care. World War II vets looked down on us," said Fujikawa, who ran his own service station for 31 years before retiring.

"Guys I knew for years — I only found out after he died, 'He was in the Korean War.'

"My dad said, 'Don't bring shame on the family.' We took that as a creed to do our best, no matter what the situation," he said.

"I'm proud I served. We faced prejudice, but did OK."

Hiroshi H. Miyamura

"It all happens for a reason."

New Mexico, it seems, does not forget its veterans. A visitor may miss the Veterans Monument in Santa Fe, the bronze monument in the Taos town square or the Vietnam Veterans Memorial State Park at Angel Fire, in the mountains above Taos. But it is hard to miss the solemn, black POW/MIA flag that accompanies the Stars and Stripes atop nearly every flagpole across the state.

Two hours west of Albuquerque, the small city of Gallup has its own monuments. The famed Navajo Code Talkers of World War II meet regularly at the Gallup Visitors Center, near the larger-than-life bronze Code Talker by the railroad station. Other Gallup honors — a park, street and high school — are personal, dedicated to Hiroshi H. Miyamura, a native son, and the sole Nisei Medal of Honor recipient of the Korean War.

Medal of Honor celebrity is hard to avoid in a small town like Gallup, but for years Hershey (as he is known to all) did his best, driven by his family obligations and his desire to put the past behind him. Like many other soldiers, he did not talk about the war with his own children.

"My kids were never curious enough to ask about the medal, but they knew about it from their friends," said the gregarious veteran. "I never attended any veterans' events. I didn't want to talk about it. I wanted to forget about it."

Drafted in 1944, Miyamura was assigned to the all-Nisei 100th Battalion at Camp Shelby, and after training ordered to combat in Europe.

"They called seven of us off the train — the government passed a law you had to be 19 to go overseas. I was 18," he said. He set off again with a later group of replacements, but the war ended five days before he arrived in Italy.

"It all happens for a reason," he offered.

Miyamura passed a few peaceful years in Gallup before being recalled for the Korean War.

"We flew to Japan and trained in the mountains in Kyushu, where my family is from. The first guy I meet is a 17-year-old kid from Boston named Joe Annello."

The two would never forget each other. In a few months' time, Miyamura would save Annello's life.

"We landed at Wonson and had to fight up to North Korea to the Yalu River, then we covered the retreat to Hungnam. In April 1951, we were sent north of Seoul and told to dig in and hold at all costs. The Chinese hit us April 24th, 1951."

Miyamura's machine gun platoon was clearly outnumbered and about to be overrun. He ordered his men back but stayed himself to defend their withdrawal. He fought into the night with a machine gun, grenades and his knife. Wounded, he crawled away, passed out and awoke as a prisoner of war. He joined other POWs in a long march into captivity. Those who fell behind were shot or bayoneted. His buddy Joe was in the group. Miyamura was badly wounded, but Annello was worse, wounded in both legs and losing much blood. Annello swears Miyamura picked him up and carried him 10 miles, saving his life. Miyamura says it wasn't that far.

The men separated, and both later assumed the other had died. Annello was soon rescued from a small POW camp, while Miyamura spent 20 months in captivity, weighing less than 100 pounds when eventually freed. While a captive, Miyamura was secretly awarded the Medal of Honor for saving his men from certain death or capture. News of the award was kept quiet to shield him from possible mistreatment as a prisoner. When he was released, President Eisenhower presented him with the medal.

Ecstatic, Joe Annello saw the photo in a newspaper. The men reconnected and, ever since, have been as close as brothers.

"People never know what they will do under the circumstances," Miyamura said. "Most times, you don't have time to think.

"I was trying to be a hero, sending the guys back. And they all made it back."

Ted Oye

"I was in uniform, but no one would give me a job."

Ted Oye left home as a boy; a lifetime later, he returned a man. In between, he spent a long career far across the country and four years in the U.S. Army with the 442nd Regimental Combat Team.

His father had died in 1934, and Ted's older brother Gary was supporting the family that included their mom, sister Terri, and younger brother, Tosh. As soon as they were old enough, Ted and Gary spent several summers working in a salmon cannery in Alaska to make money, more than they could in Seattle. When Gary, the provider, was called to the draft, Ted stepped up instead and took his place. He had barely turned 21.

He said he was the only Asian in basic training at Camp Robinson, Arkansas.

"At the end of training, the Caucasians all went one way, and I went to Camp Crowder."

There he worked for the quartermaster as a laborer, loading trucks and doing kitchen work.

"I didn't get a letter from my family for quite a while," Ted remembers. "Then I got a letter they were in Minidoka. Where is Minidoka?"

His family had been ordered to the Puyallup Assembly Center, and then sent to the Minidoka Relocation Center in Idaho.

"When I found out, I thought I was the lucky one to be in the Army."

Ted was promoted to corporal and sent to Camp Shelby, Mississippi, for cadre training, and later assigned to 3rd Battalion's Headquarters Company, to an anti-tank platoon outfitted with three 57 mm guns. Earlier 37 mm guns had proved too small to be effective; the bigger ones were only a bit better. Ted was in charge of one gun and trained the eight men under him.

The 2nd and 3rd Battalions joined the 100th Battalion, already fighting in Italy. There, the hilly terrain and the lack of targets limited the usefulness of the anti-tank guns. At first, Ted and his mostly Hawaiian gun crew manned roadblocks, but most of the war, the men helped the medics and acted as litter bearers. Unlike medics, they carried rifles and wore no red crosses on their helmets. The men first encountered the infamous German 88 artillery near Sorvieto.

"Guys were cheering and crowding around a farmhouse on top of a hill. The Germans were on the opposite hill and saw them. That was our initiation. The 88s were deadly."

Promoted again to staff sergeant, Ted and his men were deployed to L and I Companies, as they were needed. They were in France with L Company on an overnight mission led by Maj. Emmet L. O'Connor. The O'Connor Task Force circled around the Germans and, the next morning, caught the enemy in a pincer movement against the advancing 2nd Battalion and artillery fire from the 522nd. The bold action earned the 442nd one of its seven Presidential Unit Citations.

Still worse, Ted said, were the battles for Bruyères and, a few days later, for the Lost Battalion. He remembers when enemy machine gunners set up a crossfire at a bend in the road.

"They hit my helmet, put a big hole in the helmet and creased my head. A few seconds or maybe a minute later, I crawled downhill and got away."

His friend Micky Ogata was surprised to see him at the 50th reunion.

"Ted, I thought you were dead! I found your helmet with a hole in it."

Ted earned the Bronze Star and Purple Heart in the woods outside Bruyères. He didn't know the hell he lived through was an effort to save the Lost Battalion until the rescued men started crawling out of their foxholes.

Ted served with the 442nd through the Champagne Campaign, the return to Italy, the assault on the Gothic line and the Po Valley Campaign. When the war ended, he guarded German POWs in Livorno, Italy.

"I was discharged early, in November 1945, the day before Thanksgiving, at Fort Dix, New Jersey. My family had relocated nearby to Philadelphia. I had no reason to go back to Seattle. I met my wife, Sunkie, in Philadelphia, and we married June 29, 1947.

"I was in uniform, but no one would give me a job. They would just look at my face and wouldn't even give me an interview. I didn't think it was prejudice, but now …" His voice trailed off.

Ted and his wife moved to Vineland, New Jersey, where he took over a jewelry business. A Rotarian convention took him and his family to Japan, where he found relatives in Fukuoka and began corresponding and visiting back and forth. He retired in 1990, and although their many friends were in New Jersey, Ted and Sunkie found themselves drawn to Seattle to be near their family. It took him almost 50 years, but Ted had gone home again.

George Masuda

"When you were in, you were in."

The room was dark and unremarkable; only a few Army medals and tarnished bronze trophies distinguished it from so many others. George Masuda sat in the darkness. He explained he had not adjusted to the loss of his wife. It had been a few months, not long enough for the melancholy to pass. Sadness filled his voice, filled the dark room.

A question about a boxing trophy seemed to stir his enthusiasm. He had been a leading member of the Sacramento High School boxing team, possessing considerable skills by the time he graduated from the old high school in 1936. By 1942, he was a bantamweight fighter for the United States Army. One silver trophy bore an "8" on a blue field, representing, he explained, the Army 8th Division. Though well into his 80s, it was not hard to imagine Masuda as a younger man and a championship boxer.

"My draft status was 1-A, so I enlisted July 8, 1941," he remembered. "You were told to report to South Side Park at Sixth Street, and when you were in, you were in — you couldn't go home. Army pay was $21 a month."

An overnight train took the recruits to the Presidio of Monterey, and after 10 days, another train carried them east to Texas for basic training. Masuda was later assigned to Fort Jackson, South Carolina. It was there his Army boxing career took off. Every Monday night he competed downtown in three, three-minute rounds, cheered on by an arena full of fellow soldiers.

"I was in the 13th Infantry, and every unit had a boxing team: the 121st Infantry, the 28th Infantry, the engineers."

The fact that he routinely won must have been noticed by his superiors.

Masuda said, "In February, I was made a corporal, and in June, a sergeant. I had been in the Army 11 months. Some regular Army guys were in three or four years and they were just Pfcs.!"

He attended Army administration school and was assigned to personnel. The 13th Infantry participated in maneuvers in Tennessee and moved on to California for desert training, leaving Masuda behind — by then Japanese Americans could not go to California. He began to see Japanese American soldiers coming in, "a few at a time," and being sent to the Military Intelligence Service, or to the infantry as replacements for the 100th/442nd. Masuda was sent to training at the Army Pharmacy School in El Paso, Texas.

In one transit between bases, he got off the train in Sacramento and walked around for a couple hours, seeing all the Japanese American businesses boarded up. The next move surprised him: from El Paso, he was transferred to Fort Lawton, Washington, a major way station for troops heading to the Pacific.

"But there was a War Department directive, no Japanese Americans go to the Pacific," he said. "I stood on the deck, expecting to be called off the ship. Instead, they sent me to Tinian, to set up a hospital for the casualties they expected from the invasion of Japan. I was there when the atomic bombs dropped. Then we got the word, Japan had had enough.

"I had four sisters, and three of them were still in camp, first at Tule Lake, then at Topaz. The fourth went to Minnesota when her husband joined the MIS. I went to visit them once — it was minus five degrees! My parents were still in camp, so I volunteered for Japan and spent four and a half months at the 309th General Hospital on Kyushu."

Masuda said he experienced no racism in the service.

Returning to Sacramento after the war, he worked for over 30 years for the State of California. Pondering Fate, or more likely, Army logic (the same logic that sent him to service in the Pacific), he recalled another local hero, Tom Takata.

"I went into the service with this fellow, Tom. We were in the 8th Division together, and then he went to the 121st Regiment and, later, the 442nd," Masuda said.

While Masuda fought in the ring, collecting his trophies, another Sacramento boy fought in Europe, coming home with only a Purple Heart. Losing some enthusiasm, Masuda seemed not regretful, but pensive, leaving certain things unsaid.

Frank Isogawa

"I could fix anything, build anything, drive anything."

Fig farming is on its way out. One Fresno farmer after another has sold out to developers. Frank Isogawa now lives on former farmland south of the city. Frank is an Army veteran and longtime officer of his VFW Post. As he drives back and forth from his neat, ranch-style house, he passes through suburban neighborhoods and strip malls replacing the orchards, raisins and cotton that not long ago defined the region. Frank looks younger than his 88 years. He doesn't complain, but a certain sadness shows on his face and in his voice.

Frank's father, Joe (Joichi), planted many acres of fig orchards, working with Japanese and Chinese crews who dynamited a hole in the local hardpan for each seedling. Joe Isogawa came to the United States in the 1890s. Although educated in Japan, he only found work as a laborer on railroads in Idaho and Wyoming. Because he read Chinese and learned English, Joichi could communicate between the workers and their employers, and he soon advanced to a better job as timekeeper. After the 1906 San Francisco earthquake, Joe moved to the Central Valley and put his skills to work as a labor contractor.

Frank and his brothers, Hiro, Ben and Tom, all served in the Army during or after World War II. Their family, like all Japanese American families in California, was forced out of the state during the war, abandoning their home and livelihood for confinement in the Jerome, Arkansas, internment camp. Frank was deemed unfit to serve in the wartime military because of his Japanese ancestry. While locked up at Jerome, he worked on radios in the camp repair shop.

"Growing up, we didn't even have a radio in our house — we couldn't afford one until I built one myself."

Irony caught up with Frank when he was finally drafted *after* the war ended, he said, but a physical exam revealed a hearing problem that might have ended his military service.

"Around 1940, a man stuck his arm out a car window and shot at me, and the bullet went right by my ear," he said, using his finger to trace a line from his ear past the corner of his mouth. "I couldn't hear a damn thing out of my damn right ear. They tried to kick me out of basic training until I took a Signal Corps test and made one of the highest scores," he said.

"The Army didn't give me any training on repairing radios, but I could fix anything, build anything, drive anything — if you grew up on a farm you could do that. I served in Livorno, Italy, repairing radios at the Signal Corps depot. I got back to the States in May 1947."

Frank and other veterans soon chartered a VFW Post for Fresno's Nisei veterans. He served as Commander of Post 8499 for 14 years and as Adjutant for another 16. A dozen Post members formed an honor guard, providing ceremonial firing squads for veterans' burials. He said they served at 300 burials a year through the 1990s.

"We would drive to Santa Nella, to the San Joaquin Valley National Cemetery, and attend every funeral, at least two or three each day. The most was eight in a day — and we did that several times. Sometimes we would do two funerals in Fresno, drive over to Clovis and do two more. We aren't called much these days, and anyway, now we have trouble getting enough guys."

Frank described his Post members, many World War II veterans — pride evident in his voice as he recalled heroes with Bronze and Silver Stars and memorable experiences. Some suffered devastating wounds. Tom Sano, his brother-in-law and a 100th Battalion veteran, bore a large circular scar stretching from his hip across his back.

"It looked like hamburger," Frank said. "I think he smothered a grenade in Italy, that's the only thing that would make that scar. He wouldn't say how he got wounded, only that they were going to put him in for a Silver Star because they knew they wouldn't give a Nisei the Medal of Honor."

After a lengthy hospital stay, Sano rejoined the 100th in southern France to find not a single familiar face in his unit. There was no one left to write him up for a medal — all were either dead, or wounded and evacuated. Fighting at Biffontaine alongside his new comrades, he took two bullets through the knee. Sano's knee bothered him the rest of his life, and even into the 1990s, shrapnel still worked itself out through his skin.

"He couldn't raise his arm, he couldn't work or climb a ladder, and the V.A. didn't give him nothing," Frank said.

Edgar Hamasu

"There was no victory for us — there was no peace."

A relentless wind blew outside Edgar Hamasu's mountainside home, from which one could see down to the Pacific and the landmark Diamondhead, in all its squat, brown volcanic glory. Volunteering for the military at a young age, Hamasu served with the Military Intelligence Service during the Korean War. He is president of Hawaii's MIS Veterans Club.

Like many Japanese Americans in pre–World War II Hawaii, Hamasu grew up in modest surroundings, on a 10-acre coffee farm his parents leased from a sugar plantation. His parents later began working at the plantation because the coffee farm was not productive, he explained, and there were seven kids to feed.

"I came from the country, and we were very poor; maybe everyone was during the Depression. My childhood was happy, but I was always hungry. From age 13, we worked in the sugarcane field. We had so much debt to the plantation store and the little Tahara Store! After ninth grade at Honokaa School, my oldest brother and sister had to go to work at the plantation."

His childhood changed abruptly with the Pearl Harbor attack.

"The owner of Tahara Store was picked up by the FBI and sent to Sand Island. Mr. Tahara must have had a weak heart because he died there while his two sons were in the 442nd Regiment, fighting in Europe. They did not lock up Rev. Higa since he was a Christian, but even in our small area, five or six people were picked up, including Mr. and Mrs. Suzuki, our Japanese language school teachers," Hamasu said.

Drastic changes were also in store for Ed's future wife, Helen Tanabe. She and her family were removed from their 80-acre Marysville, California, rice farm and interned with other West Coast Japanese Americans. They left their home and farm with a bumper rice crop in the field.

Hamasu's older brother, Mitsuo (also called "Ted"), was already in the Army, one of the first draftees. He was serving in the Territorial Guard at the time of Pearl Harbor, when Japanese Americans were ordered to turn in their weapons. Later, Ted joined the 100th Battalion, landed at Salerno and fought in the fierce battle at Monte Cassino. At age 92, he still suffers from severe trench foot.

"Ted sent photos of the snow in Camp McCoy, and of the Statue of Liberty in New York," Edgar remembers. "And he always sent us an allotment of $20 to $25 each month. All during the war, we had a photo of him at the head of the table, and at each meal, we placed some rice and food in front of it. *Kamisama* is a Shinto god. If you die in battle, your soul becomes part of God. This makes death in battle bittersweet.

"I heard so much about the heroism of the 100th and 442nd, so I volunteered the same year I graduated high school. After basic training at Fort Ord, I was assigned to Presidio of Monterey Army Language School. There were nine or 10 of us in class, all Japanese Americans. When I graduated, I had accumulated a 30-day furlough and planned to head home to help my parents for a while. But on the Army transport ship to Hawaii, we learned about the Korean War.

"June 25th, 1950, is still indelible in my mind — the start of the Korean War. They needed interpreters. My furlough was cut to seven days, and they flew us directly from Hickam Air Base to Hanada Airfield in Japan. Less than a month after the Inchon Landing, four officers and four enlisted men, including me, flew to Kimpo Airfield — the main airfield in South Korea near Seoul — and we interrogated POWs for tactical info, as many of them spoke Japanese.

"MacArthur's strategy was to cut the North Koreans' long supply line to Pusan, and it worked — the North Koreans retreated en masse, and there were many POWs. Here I was, just a sergeant, 19 years old, interrogating enemy colonels and lieutenant colonels," he recalled. "We moved up and down Korea as the war moved up and down. It was a stalemate. There was no victory for us — there was no peace.

"My hope is that the Koreans find peace — that's what I think most South Koreans want. I don't know if it will be in my lifetime …

"We didn't see each other, but all three sons in my family were in the U.S. Army in Korea at the same time. I served for three years and six months. When I got out, I took up city planning, which may reflect my idealism. That's the feeling of Japanese Americans, true optimists. No matter how bad it looks, things will get better."

Frank J. Tanaka

"I had nightmares for 50 years."

Stairs lead up to the modest VFW office on the second floor of a suburban community center, where a well-worn desk is covered with many papers but little adornment, save a simple sign:

FRANK TANAKA
PERPETUAL COMMANDER

Smiling Frank Tanaka has led his VFW Post off and on for 50 years but says he will soon retire.

"I'd rather be out fishing *now*, but they've already told me, when I retire, that's it, no one else will take over as commander."

He pilots his chair back and forth, swiveling left and right to point out the room's few items of interest, and begins his unlikely story of cowboys, honor and warriors, old and new.

"I'm a *Samurai*," he says. "The oldest son of an eldest son. My father, Yamano-oy san, owned a mountain in Japan, so they called him Mountain Man, and he was a community leader. My mother, a cultured, high-class lady, was widowed in San Francisco before she met Dad and married him."

Tanaka himself grew up far from the mountains, on cattle ranches straddling the Nebraska-Wyoming border, a region called the Sand Hills, modest swales growing taller as they lead north to become South Dakota's Black Hills. As a 10-year-old, Tanaka and a fearless mongrel he called Puppy were running the family's cattle operation — a boy and a dog lording it over 150 head of cattle. His half-brother Henry, 15 years older, took care of the farming on their 800 acres.

"Our brand was the Oh-bar-you."

O — U

"I was a Nisei cowboy. I had a horse named Trigger," he said, smiling. "Nebraska values are very similar to Samurai values. In Nebraska, you have to get along with everyone, so I had no problems with prejudice growing up. My dad was the first to settle there, and he brought other people over from Japan. I'd say 50 to 60 Japanese families lived in the area, enough that there was a school in Scottsbluff where we learned a little Japanese."

But even good Nebraska values were challenged in the days after Pearl Harbor, when the FBI began arresting the community's leading members.

"Our reverend, he was taken. Dad was a leader, and the FBI wanted him, too, until the sheriff told them, 'You're going to take him over my dead body!' "

More trouble soon followed as the family watched their 400-acre soybean crop leveled in a hailstorm.

"It completely wiped us out. That convinced my father to give up. It was the first time I saw tears in his eyes.

"Over the years, my father co-signed bank notes for many people," Tanaka said. "Some ran out on him and left him to pay their loans. When we decided to move away, the bank manager told him he didn't have to pay off one last loan, but my father insisted on paying. I had to explain to the man it was a matter of honor. The bank manager told me, 'I've never met a man like your father.' I was extremely proud of Dad. He and Mother were the most honest people you'd ever meet."

Facing the finality of the hailstorm, the family packed up and moved to California, settling at first in an orange grove near Anaheim.

"It was like the Grapes of Wrath. We lived in a trailer next to a *barrio* and some people thought I was Mexican," Tanaka said. "I had a tremendous principal, teacher and coach who all looked after me."

Not a big man, Tanaka was an athlete, and played high school football, basketball, baseball and tennis. As a senior, he captained the baseball team and was named Athlete of the Year. He graduated in 1950, about the time the Korean War broke out.

"In '52, I was drafted into the Army, and by luck of the draw I went to Korea," he said. "I was trained as a Signal Corps wireman and switchboard man, but in Korea, I became a rifleman *first*, then a wireman."

Tanaka won't talk more than that about combat, and he explained why: "I had nightmares for 50 years," he said.

Returning from Korea, he studied landscape architecture but was forced to abandon school in order to care for his mother. Instead, he began a landscaping business, which he ran with his keen set of values.

"You serve your clients, not the money," he explained.

For all his accomplishments — his beautiful gardens, a successful business and an enduring leadership position among veterans — Tanaka has his own measure of success: the wellbeing of one of his employees, a man Tanaka helped through a personal tragedy and taught the same values that guided him all these years.

"My parents brought me up by the Samurai code," the Nisei cowboy said modestly. "I lived by it. I still do today."

Mas Masuda

"Three buddies ... all three were killed."

The minivans had left the Fountain Valley, California school driveway, and the last kids were shuffling away under the weight of their backpacks. A departing teacher smiled as she held open the door for two visitors, the diminutive senior citizen, trailed by a bearded man hoisting his own backpack.

Once inside, they saw the photos of the man's brother displayed prominently in the entryway. The school principal strode purposefully toward the two.

"Can I help you?" She then recognized the older man, Mr. Masuda. "Oh, hi. Good to see you. Take all the time you want."

Masao Masuda had led this tour many times. His brother Kazuo had been killed in action and Kazuo Masuda Middle School was named after him. So was a nearby VFW post. Kazuo is a local hero — no, he is a hero.

One of four brothers to serve in the Army during World War II, Mas told about his famous younger brother and his family that became famous as well.

Later at home, Mas, an MIS veteran, passed photo albums around the table. He had a copy of the same photo of Kazuo in his dress uniform and one of a gathering of Army officers, press and the Masuda family on the porch of their farmhouse. A photo of three Nisei in Army uniforms made him pause.

"Three buddies, Abraham Ohama, Kaz Masuda and George Akiyama. All three were killed."

Mas said Kazuo was already in the Army when the family was sent into internment at the Jerome, Arkansas, War Relocation Center. Assigned to the newly formed 442nd, Kazuo joined F Company and sailed overseas to the fighting in Italy.

In the fierce combat that followed the battle for Hill 140, he carried out his own plan to repulse a German assault that was pinning down his unit. Kazuo advanced by himself, carrying a mortar tube and ammunition. He filled his helmet with dirt, fashioning a makeshift stand for the base of the mortar. Then, holding and aiming the tube with one hand, he loaded and fired mortar rounds with the other. When he ran through his ammunition, he crawled back for more and resumed his barrage. The rain of mortar shells forced the enemy's withdrawal. Masuda returned to his lines uninjured, and was soon decorated for his bravery and initiative with a Distinguished Service Cross.

A month later, Kazuo saved his men again, exposing himself to enemy fire to allow the others to withdraw to a safer position. This time he was killed, and buried in a GI cemetery in Italy.

Within two months, a second brother, Takashi, was hit by shrapnel in the Lost Battalion battle. (Another family casualty, Mas's brother-in-law, Takaji Goto, was severely wounded while serving in the 442nd.)

The Jerome War Relocation Center was the last to open and the first to close. Daughter Mary Masuda received permission to travel in advance of her family to survey the condition of the farm, making the trip alone. A group of men approached her, saying her family should not return.

"Japs are not welcome in Orange County," they told her.

This made news: a decorated war hero's family threatened for wanting to return to their home. What would happen when the thousands of families returned to California from incarceration?

A plan was devised by the War Relocation Authority to address the problem. Kazuo had been killed before any ceremony to present his Distinguished Service Cross. Famed Army General Joseph W. Stilwell was chosen to present the commendation to Kazuo's family.

Medals going to next-of-kin are traditionally presented to the soldier's mother. In Kazuo's case, this was not possible. Military medals could only be awarded to U.S. citizens, and Tamae Masuda was not a citizen. Instead, Gen. Stilwell pinned the medal on Mary Masuda, who, in turn, pinned it on her mother. From the Masuda farm, Stilwell then traveled to the Santa Ana Bowl, a nearby stadium, to address a larger audience. So did an Army captain, future President Ronald Reagan.

"The blood that has soaked the sands of a beach is all one color," Reagan said. "America stands unique in the world: the only country not founded on race, but on an ideal … That is the American Way."

The saga did not end with Reagan's words. After the war, Kazuo's body came home from the military cemetery in Italy, but his burial was refused by a local cemetery. After some discussion, the cemetery relented but, following a restrictive covenant, would only allow burial in a less than desirable location, one reserved for Japanese.

"Hometown Cemetery Bars Burial of Nisei War Hero," headlined the *Pacific Citizen*. The cemetery relented once again, and the hero was laid to rest with military honors.

Terry Nakanishi

"Wacs did the same work the men did!"

In a house on a hill above Monterey, California, the animated, gray-haired lady turned her back on the bay view and became very serious.

"Don't put anything about me in there," said World War II veteran Terry Nakanishi. "I'd like you to write about all the Nisei women who attended the MIS school at Fort Snelling. They are the ones who deserve the credit."

The former Wac was being modest. She was one of those pictured in the many photographs on her dining room table, her pretty face prominent in the sea of khaki-clad women. Like the others, she volunteered for service during World War II.

"I wanted to make a difference," she said.

"I was born in Idaho and raised in Idaho and Montana. Of course, we were the only Asians. I never experienced discrimination growing up, never heard the word 'Jap.'

"I had just graduated high school and was looking for work when the war broke out. When I heard about Pearl Harbor, I thought, what in the world is going to happen to us? My parents said, 'You can't help it. *Shikata ga nai.* If they tell us we have to go, we must go.' I knew my brothers would be in the Army and fighting our relatives over there," Nakanishi said.

"After Pearl Harbor, my father immediately lost his job on the Union Pacific railroad, like all the other Japanese. He had worked for the railroad for 40 years and was almost eligible for a pension, so when they fired him, they gave him a partial pension. I wanted to go to nursing school and needed to make some money. No one was hiring Japanese. I could do steno or secretarial work, but the only work I could get was in the potato field, or housework, of course. That paid five dollars a week."

Idaho was beyond the Exclusion Zone, meaning its few Japanese American families were not sent into internment camps. But Nakanishi said her parents might have been better off in a camp.

"For a while, they had to sleep in the car. In camp, at least they would have had a roof over their heads."

Wanting to do her part for the war effort, she went down to the recruiting office to enlist in the Air Corps. She was turned down. She tried the Marines, then the Women's Army Corps, WAC.

"I gave up after they said they weren't taking Japanese. They were polite; they said they would call me when things changed.

"My mother and I ended up working in the potato fields. We had to lift the heavy baskets, dump the potatoes into gunnysacks, then stack them in rows for the trucks to pick up.

"Finally, March 6, 1944, I was allowed to enlist in the Women's Army Corps. Basic training at Fort Des Moines was rough! Our day started at 5:00 a.m. We did everything the men did, everything except handle weapons. Only one other Nisei was in basic training with me, Miyo Sadahiro. She was my bunkmate. I asked for a medical assignment after finishing basic, since I thought it would help me in nursing school, but they assigned me to Ordnance, working in a warehouse. That's how the Army works. But it was interesting work, and I thought I was doing my part. We were replacing the men so they could go to combat.

"In the late fall, 1944, I was stationed at Fort Benjamin Harrison, Indiana, when I was sent to Fort Snelling, to the language school. We didn't even know they were organizing a detachment there. They came around and took all the girls with Oriental faces and sent us to Fort Snelling — even a Chinese girl who didn't speak any Japanese. You had to be 5'1" to get in the WAC, and I was one of the tallest at Snelling at 5'3". Our day started at 6:00, and studies went until 9:00 at night. Our barracks was an old hospital annex. And it was cold! I felt sorry for the girls from Hawaii. There were a couple Caucasians, one was a missionary's daughter, who already spoke some Japanese.

"When we arrived at Snelling, our CO told us there was a dance that night at the field house. We called it tap dancing. One man would tap another's shoulder to dance with a girl. One soldier from Hilo, Lefty, kept breaking in to dance with me, and he ignored the other taps all night. Then he asked to walk me back to the barracks. He was getting ready to ship out. We saw each other and he wanted to get married. I said no, we only knew each other two months. Lefty asked to call my parents in Idaho, and he spoke with them a long time. They liked him. They weren't used to Nisei boys speaking Japanese. They told me, 'Don't let this boy get away!'"

On January 2, 1945, Toyome "Terry" Uyeno and Toshio "Lefty" Nakanishi were married in the Fort Snelling chapel. The post newspaper headline read "Two U.S. Japs Wed."

Lefty shipped to the Pacific a month later, serving to the end of the war. He stayed in the Army and served in post-war

Japan. Terry was one of 13 Wacs selected to duty at General Headquarters Japan, leaving for Tokyo on January 27, 1946.

"Tokyo was devastated! Oh, the children begging, and people living under cardboard! We were unprepared for what we saw.

"We were the first Wacs to be sent to Japan, but when we got to Tokyo, they had no place to put us and were ready to send us back. Gen. MacArthur didn't especially like the Wacs. He said, get discharged, or if you want to stay, quit the Army and we will give you civil service jobs. Of course, we were happy with civil service jobs because they paid better. The Wacs did the same work the men did, and we were getting a measly $50 a month.

"It was a year or more before they had housing for Army dependents. The only dependent was Mrs. MacArthur! Lefty transferred to Tokyo from Niigata, but for a year, he lived in Norton Hall, the dormitory for the Army CIC (Counter Intelligence Corps) people and I lived in the Hotel Shiba, which had been converted into quarters for us girls. When we moved in together, I tried to ask for an ironing board. I knew military terms in Japanese, and I could read maps, but I didn't know how to say ironing board!"

Terry quit her civil service job when her son Calvin was born and moved back to the U.S. to live with her family in Idaho until the Korean War was over. Her younger son, Gregory, was born in Pocatello.

Lefty made a career of the Army and, like others, moved his family around from one post to another. He served in Korea and two tours in Vietnam. He was troop commander and head of the Intelligence Division (G-2) at the Defense Language Institute in Monterey. He succeeded in getting a building there named "Nisei Hall," commemorating the World War II linguists. When the Army asked him about a third Vietnam tour, he decided to retire after 30 years with the rank of colonel. Terry volunteered at the nearby Fort Ord Hospital and the local Red Cross Bloodmobile.

"My older half-brother, Kiyoshi Murakami, graduated Ashton High School and went straight to Pocatello to enlist in the 442nd. For some reason he flunked the first physical, but he was determined to enlist. I don't know what he did, but he went back to the doctor and recruiter and passed the second time. He was in G Company and was killed two weeks before V-E Day in the 'final push.' I was at Fort Snelling when I got the news."

Terry and Lefty, and their families, gave much to America. Their son Calvin served in Vietnam with the 82nd Airborne Division. Lefty's three brothers also served in the MIS. Terry's half-brother Yoshito, made a career of the Army with the engineers, and, as Terry said, Kiyoshi served in the 442nd and was killed in Italy two weeks before the end of the war. Lefty died in 2002.

"I just wanted to do my part," Terry said. "We all wanted to do our part."

Norman Y. Mineta

"I saw my father cry three times."

It is hard to condense anyone's story to just a few words; it is impossible when the person is Norman Mineta.

From his political start in local government in San Jose, California, his career led to mayor, congressman, Secretary of the Interior for Democratic President Bill Clinton, and Secretary of Transportation for Republican George W. Bush. He became the first Asian American to hold nearly all of those positions. As Secretary of Transportation, he gave the order to suspend air travel over the United States on the morning of September 11th, 2001. On an all-too-rare visit to San Francisco, Mineta seemed to enjoy talking about his family's history during a light lunch in a restaurant overlooking Market Street.

His American success story began around 1902, when an uncle in Salinas, California, wrote to Mineta's grandfather in Japan: "You ought to send one of your sons over here to see American farming techniques."

The grandfather must have agreed, because at age 14, Mineta's father, Kunisaku, boarded a steamship by himself in Yokohama, sailing for California, he thought, but landing instead in Seattle.

"It took him a year and a half, working on every farm and lumber camp along the way, to make it south to Salinas," Secretary Mineta said.

The uncle insisted Kunisaku learn English and enrolled him in first grade.

"He met humility," Mineta said, chuckling. "Some of the kids were as tall as he was."

Kunisaku began working at the Spreckels sugar beet plant and, hopeful for a future in America, wrote to a friend in Japan, asking for help finding a wife. Among the photos he received was one of the friend's younger sister, Kane. Holding her photo in his hand, Kunisaku met Kane at the gangplank in San Francisco in 1912. They married at once and returned to Salinas.

After a few years, the elder Mineta's English skills and hard work paid off, and Spreckels put him in charge of a branch operation in San Jose until a long hospitalization for influenza ended his agriculture career. He opened Mineta Agency, a local office of West Coast Life Insurance Co. Back in the '20s, most insurance companies levied a surcharge on "Orientals." West Coast Life did not, according to Secretary Mineta, who years later joined his father in the business.

The family fared well during the depression and built a house in San Jose, only to be uprooted by the Relocation in 1942 and sent to Heart Mountain, Wyoming, challenging their dream and understanding of America.

"My brother cried, 'I'm an enemy alien.' Here's a kid who was born and raised in San Jose," Mineta said. "'Why is the land of my birth attacking the land of my heart?'

"I saw my father cry three times," he said. "7 December 1941, 29 May 1942 on the train to Santa Anita, where we were sent on the way to Heart Mountain." He paused. "The third time was when my mother died."

At Heart Mountain, Mineta was active in the Boy Scouts and befriended a local Wyoming scout, Alan Simpson, who became a lifelong friend and a prominent U.S. senator.

"Most Japanese Americans from San Jose spent 16 to 19 months in camp," Mineta said. "People started coming back from camp in 1946, without a pot to carry water in. The *San Jose Mercury News* wrote, 'These are our friends and neighbors coming home. Please treat them accordingly.' But homes were firebombed, and shootings happened. We had a young fellow from San Jose at the Stockton veterans hospital. He went into town for a haircut, and someone shot and killed him. This was in 1946."

Early on, Norman Mineta set his sights on a career in aviation, majoring in aeronautical engineering at the University of California, Berkeley, but "for the safety of the country," he deadpanned, changed his studies to business and transportation. The Korean War was going on. Mineta earned an ROTC commission in the U.S. Army and arrived in Korea at the end of hostilities. His 500th Military Intelligence Group debriefed North Korean and Chinese POWs before their repatriation. The 500th MI Group evolved from ATIS, Allied Translator and Interpreter Section, the World War II unit staffed by Nisei soldiers of the MIS. He served next in Japan, commanding a military intelligence detachment. His brother Albert and brother-in-law Minoru Endo also served in Army Intelligence.

Following his military service, Mineta returned to San Jose. His father encouraged him to gain some experience outside the family business, and for a while he commuted by train to work in San Francisco. He later became the first non-white agent for

Seattle's Safeco Insurance Co., but only after three interviews with the company president.

San Jose had a substantial Japanese community after World War II. Fortunately, a few Nisei began to participate in the political system to prevent future abuses of power.

"A lot of us, including me, really stood on the shoulders of those folks," he said.

Mineta began his own political career on the San Jose Human Rights Commission, then served as leader of the new Housing Commission, an important post as the city's population boomed. When he was approached about filling a vacancy on the City Council, he paused before accepting.

"I better talk to my dad," he said.

"In Japan, there's an adage about politics, my father told me. He then laced his fingers together, leaving a single digit sticking out, as he remembers his father doing.

"'Like a nail sticking out of a board — it always gets hammered,'" my father said. "'But if you can stand it, you ought to do it.'"

He served on the City Council two years before becoming vice mayor in 1969. He ran for mayor in 1971, beating out 10 other candidates and becoming the first Asian American mayor of a major American city.

Mineta received the nation's highest civilian honor, the Presidential Medal of Freedom, on retiring from public service in 2006. Of his many "firsts" and his accomplishments, he smiles while remembering his time as mayor of San Jose.

"I loved being mayor. We did a lot of good things," he said. "You make a city grow and, just like a teenager, you want it to grow gracefully."

Robert M. Wada

"Christmas in 1951 was the worst Christmas of my life."

Bob Wada prays for peace. Peace for the people of Korea, the land where he fought six decades ago; peace for dozens of combat zones where Americans fight today, or may fight tomorrow; but mostly, peace within himself. This last, the hardest to achieve.

Robert M. Wada grew up in Redlands, California, a San Bernardino Valley city, east of Los Angeles and once surrounded by miles of orchards. Redlands produced many veterans, and Wada's large family was no exception, he said.

"My two brothers, Ted and Frank, were in the 442nd in Europe. Ted, in K Company 442, re-enlisted in the 101st Airborne and was sent to Korea. My brother Henry joined the Marines in '46. No, he tried to join in '46, and they turned him down because he was Japanese. He went back in '47, and they took him. He served until '49. Then in '50, when the war started, he re-enlisted and got sent to Korea right away. He was already there when I got there. He was wounded twice and then came home.

"I joined the Marine Reserve in '48 for two years. I joined in May '48 and got out in May '50. The war started in June. If I had joined in June, I would have been in the Reserve and been gone, since all those guys got annihilated — they went to the Chosin Reservoir — but I was already discharged."

But a year into the fighting, Wada enlisted, volunteering to go to war.

"People ask me why I joined. They think I joined to prove my loyalty. It wasn't loyalty. No, at that time I was just young. I was going with this girl, Jo Ann Ideka, and she says, 'Let's get married.' I got my mother's permission because I'm underage, and we got married," Wada said.

"Right away, I called my friend Bob Madrid (I called him 'Bat') back home in Redlands, and say I am going to join the Marines. Want to go? He says yeah, and comes out, and we join together. We go to boot camp together, come home on leave, and my wife died."

He paused and took a breath.

"The Red Cross arranged for me to have two more weeks' leave, but Bob goes back to Pendleton and gets assigned to a new infantry unit. I go back two weeks later and didn't know we'd be separated. I got assigned to tanks and tried to get transferred, but they said no. But overseas, we got together and visited a couple times, me, Bob and my brother Hank.

"Then this one battle, Hill 749, I was up in the trenches with my captain observing the attack. We were coming back in a jeep, and Marines about to hit the hill next were sitting on the side of the road taking a smoke break, and I see Bat. The captain says, 'Who's that, your compadre?' Yes, sir. That's my buddy from back home. 'Go talk to him.'

"I ran over there and talked to him, shook his hand, and asked him where my brother was, and he says, 'Oh, they're coming out of that ravine over there.' I asked him if he was scared. He said, 'Well, I wasn't worried until I heard we were going to be point platoon.' I felt a chill. Point platoon is right there with the enemy. 'OK,' I said. 'Keep your head down. Don't be a hero. We'll get together when we get home.'

"A few days later I saw a casualty list. I looked up there and there's his name, first name on the list of killed. He was the first guy killed that day, that morning. I've lived with that all my life. Why did he get killed? Why did I ask him to go? It tears me apart. I lost my wife, I lost him and, in October, I lost a good friend from Texas, Vernon Todd, killed in Korea. Christmas in 1951 was the worst Christmas of my life. When I heard that song, *Silent Night*, in Korea, I looked at the sky and just cried. I couldn't fathom why I was there and what I was doing. Why are all these people dying around me? Every time I hear *Silent Night*, I cry inside.

"The way I look at it, my wife died to save my life. It sounds weird, but I've come to that salvation. Had she not died, Bob and I would have gone back together. We would have been in the same outfit, we would have been in the same battle. Now, maybe I'd still be alive, maybe I'd be sitting here, but I don't think so," he said.

"It's called the Forgotten War, but if you take the number of Japanese Americans who served in World War II and the number of KIAs, versus the Korean War, the percent of casualties is much higher in Korea. Roy Shiraga was on the side of the road, badly wounded at the Chosin Reservoir. No one stopped to help, they thought he was a Chinese. Finally, another Nisei came along who knew him. A week later, that Nisei got killed — maybe because no one knew him.

"My father died in an internment camp, so he didn't see my brothers come home from the service. My mother, when I was going to join, she was proud. 'Go over there, be brave,

don't be afraid, do your job, and don't get sick.' I'll never forget that. Isn't that a strange thing to say when your son is going to war? Not, don't get killed, but don't get sick — because I won't be there to take care of you.

"I didn't join because I felt I owed it anybody. All I frankly joined for was to experience the war. After World War II ended, I had the feeling of being left out, of not experiencing the war. I wasn't going to stay home and say, yeah, my brothers served but I didn't.

"If I had known then what I know now, I would have still gone, but I would not have asked my friend to go. I'd do everything the same, only I wouldn't call him."

Harry Ikeda   U.S. Army   Korean War

Kats Nakatani   U.S. Army   Korean War

Larry Yamaguchi   U.S. Army   Korean War

Index of Veterans

About the Author

Tom Graves is a professional writer and photographer, shooting corporate, advertising and editorial photography for leading companies and publications. In the last decade, Tom has photographed and interviewed over 250 veterans, and his work has been exhibited at San Francisco City Hall, Webster University, National Japanese American Historical Society, Fort Knox, American Legion National Convention, Manzanar National Historic Site, National Steinbeck Center, the Presidio of San Francisco and other venues. Tom speaks extensively at veterans' events. He has developed a special bond with the Nisei veterans and a commitment to telling their story. He is a founding board member of the 99th Infantry Battalion (Separate) WWII Educational Foundation, which preserves and shares the history of another unique WWII unit. Tom also serves as historian of the Joe Rosenthal Chapter of the USMC Combat Correspondents Association.

TwiceHeroes.com features more of Tom's portraits and interviews, as well as Nisei history and recommended reading for those who want to learn more about the Nisei veterans.

Contact the author with your questions and comments, and to inquire about exhibits, presentations and photography assignments. tom@tomgraves.com • www.tomgraves.com